ADB Institute Series on Development Economics

Series Editor
Naoyuki Yoshino
Tokyo
Japan

Asia and the Pacific has been advancing in many aspects of its development, but the potential for growth is vast. The ADB Institute Series on Development Economics aims to identify and propose solutions using a multidisciplinary approach to important development issues facing economies in the Asia and Pacific region. Through edited volumes and monographs, the series showcases the research output of the Asian Development Bank Institute as well as its collaboration with other leading think tanks and institutions worldwide.

The current focus of the series is infrastructure development; financial inclusion, regulation, and education; housing policy; central and local government relations; macroeconomic policy; and governance. The series also examines the major bottlenecks to greater stability and integration in Asia and the Pacific, while addressing timely issues including trends in microfinance, fiscal policy stability, and ways of tackling income inequality. The publications in the series are relevant for scholars, policymakers, and students of economics, and provide recommendations for economic policy enhancement and a greater understanding of the implications of further capacity building and development reform in Asia and the Pacific.

More information about this series at http://www.springer.com/series/13512

ADB Institute
Financial Services Agency, Japan
International Monetary Fund Regional Office
for Asia and the Pacific
Editors

Financial System Stability, Regulation, and Financial Inclusion

Springer

Editors
ADB Institute
Chiyoda-ku
Tokyo
Japan

International Monetary Fund
Regional Office for Asia and the Pacific
Chiyoda-ku
Tokyo
Japan

Financial Services Agency, Japan
Chiyoda-ku
Tokyo
Japan

ISBN 978-4-431-56413-3 ISBN 978-4-431-55254-3 (eBook)
DOI 10.1007/978-4-431-55254-3
Springer Tokyo Heidelberg New York Dordrecht London

Printed on acid-free paper

Springer is part of Springer Science+Business Media (www.springer.com)

Preface

In light of the current global financial and economic situation, financial authorities face a number of key challenges, including maintaining financial stability; managing sovereign risk; ensuring long-term finance for stable economic growth; promoting greater access to financial services for both households and small and medium-sized enterprises (SMEs); and fostering a competitive financial industry. Striking the appropriate balance in achieving these objectives through financial supervision and regulation is an important policy issue for financial regulators. This book provides the record of a joint conference organized by the Asian Development Bank Institute (ADBI), the Financial Services Agency, Japan (FSA), and the International Monetary Fund (IMF) Regional Office for Asia and the Pacific on the topic "Financial System Stability, Financial Regulation, and Financial Inclusion," held on 27 January 2014 in Tokyo.

The global financial crisis of 2007–2009 and its aftermath focused attention on possible trade-offs between financial stability and moves to increase competition in the financial sector, which was the topic of the first session of the conference. Increased competition in the financial sector is generally found to be positive for economic growth, but can also undermine economic stability due to excessive risk-taking and too-light regulation. Increased cross-border banking activity can raise thorny issues of coordination of regulation and bank resolution. One unintended consequence of regulatory developments after the global financial crisis was increased concentration in the financial sector as a result of mergers and bank closures, which has the potential to increase problems associated with "too-big-to-fail" and moral hazard. Finally, there is a concern that higher requirements for capital adequacy and liquidity in banking and other financial sectors as a result of Basel III rules will exert a drag on economic growth.

The second session focused on access to finance for SMEs. A particular feature of Asian economies is the importance of SMEs, especially in terms of employment, and their strong needs for funds. However, SMEs face difficulties in raising funds compared to large firms, as the lack of financial data makes banks reluctant to lend to them. Limited access to trade finance also makes it more difficult for SMEs to export. Therefore, it is extremely important to reduce the information asymmetry by expanding access to credit information, and thereby facilitate SMEs' access to stable, long-term finance. Policy measures to ensure smooth financing of SMEs are critical for Asia's strong and sustainable economic growth.

The Credit Risk Database in Japan is a good example of a credit information infrastructure offering comprehensive financial data on SMEs, and there is much scope for Asian countries to develop credit databases of similar coverage and depth. Credit guarantees for SMEs are another way of facilitating SME finance by alleviating credit risks of banks and have been actively pursued in many Asian countries. However, unduly generous guarantees can create moral hazard and delay the needed restructuring of nonviable firms. An appropriate balance of risk sharing between banks and credit guarantee corporations should be established.

The third session covered issues related to the nexus of financial inclusion, financial stability, and financial education. Enhanced access to finance has two aspects: financing for small businesses and poorer households, but also access to financial services for their financial investment and asset management. The Asian region generally still falls short in both aspects. Postal savings and/or agricultural banks can play an important role in enhancing financial inclusion. Financial regulators must also grapple with possible trade-offs between financial inclusion and financial stability. On the positive side, increased access to savings can provide a larger and more stable source of funding for banks, and the risk characteristics of loans to smaller entities are generally more benign than those of large borrowers, as the latter are characterized by fat tail risks. However, deterioration of lending standards could increase systemic risk, and new categories of financial institutions need to have appropriate frameworks for supervision and regulation.

The session also discussed a range of educational programs designed to enhance financial literacy. Financial education for SMEs and individuals can have a substantial impact on their ability to use financial services wisely and prudently, but is lacking in many developing countries. The kind of programs for financial education available to enhance financial literacy and the way forward were also discussed.

We believe that the presentations and discussions of this conference provide valuable insights into ways to expand financial inclusion and deepen financial development in Asia while at the same time maintaining financial stability. We hope that this record will prove useful for policy makers, financial market regulators, and academics working on these issues.

Naoyuki Yoshino
Dean and CEO
Asian Development Bank Institute, and
Chief Advisor, Financial Research Center (FSA Institute)
Financial Services Agency, Government of Japan

Odd Per Brekk
Director
Regional Office for Asia and the Pacific
International Monetary Fund

Contents

About the Authors

Akira Ariyoshi is Professor, School of International and Public Policy, Hitotsubashi University. Prior to moving to the academia in April 2010, Mr. Ariyoshi accumulated extensive experience in the Government of Japan and international financial institutions in macroeconomic and financial policies, including as Assistant Director of Monetary and Exchange Affairs Department and Director of the Regional Office for Asia and the Pacific of the IMF, Deputy Vice-Minister for International Affairs at the Japanese Ministry of Finance and Director of the Legal and Planning Division at the Japanese Financial Services Agency. He is a graduate of Tokyo University and holds a DPhil from Oxford University.

Odd Per Brekk a Norwegian national, has been the Director of the IMF Regional Office for Asia and the Pacific since July 2013. Mr. Brekk joined the IMF in 1987 and has held several senior positions in the European and Asia and Pacific Departments, including mission chief to Indonesia and Lithuania, and Senior Resident Representative in Turkey and the Russian Federation. During 2005–2009, he was the Advisor to the First Deputy Managing Director. Earlier in his career, he worked in the African and Central Banking Departments of the IMF. Before joining the IMF, he was a senior economist at the Bank of Norway. He holds a graduate degree in economics from the University of Oslo.

Tomoyuki Furusawa joined the Ministry of Finance in April 1986 after graduating from the Law Faculty of the University of Tokyo. Between 2011 and 2013, he was in charge of designing Japanese financial market regulations including insider-trading regulations and over-the-counter derivatives reforms as Director of the Financial Markets Division at the Financial Services Agency, Japan (FSA). Since July 2013, he has been Director of the Policy and Legal Division, Planning and Coordination Bureau, FSA.

Muliaman D. Hadad has served as the Chairman of the Financial Services Agency of Indonesia since July 2012. Prior to his current position, he was Deputy Governor of Bank Indonesia (Central Bank of Indonesia) from December 2006 onward. Before joining the Financial Services Agency of Indonesia, he also held various positions in Bank Indonesia, among others as Head of the Financial System Stability Bureau since 2003 and Director of Banking Research and Regulation since 2005. His career at Bank Indonesia spanned 25 years. He currently also serves as Chair of the Indonesia Sharia Economic Community, an active manager at the Indonesia Economist Association, and as lecturer in various universities in Jakarta, Indonesia. He has been published in many scientific journals domestically and internationally and has been a speaker in numerous international forums on financial system regulation and stability. He holds a bachelor's degree in economics from the University of Indonesia (Universitas Indonesia/UI) and an MPA from John F. Kennedy School of Government, Harvard University in the United States. He earned his doctorate degree in business and economics from Monash University, Melbourne, Australia, in 1996.

Ranee Jayamaha is currently the Chairperson of Hatton National Bank PLC, the second largest private bank in Sri Lanka and Advisor to the President of Sri Lanka on banking. She received her PhD from the University of Bradford and an MSc from University of Stirling in the United Kingdom. She was Deputy Governor of the Central Bank of Sri Lanka from 2004 to 2009. During this period, she was the Chairperson of the Financial System Stability Committee, the Credit Information Bureau of Sri Lanka, the National Payments Council, the South Asian Association for Regional Cooperation Payments Council, and the Safeguard Assessment Committee. She was a member of the Monetary Policy Committee, the Sri Lanka Insurance Board, the Securities and Exchange Commission, the Working Group on General Payment System Development of the Bank for International Settlements, the Advisory Committee of the G8 Remittances Working Group, and the Safeguard Assessment Policy Review 2010 of the IMF. She has over 40 years of experience in the fields of economics, banking, finance, and regulation. In November 2012, the University of Stirling bestowed her the Degree of Doctor of the University (DUniv) in recognition of her distinguished career as one of the university's first master's graduates in economics and as a person of great distinction in the fields of learning the arts and public affairs.

Akihiko Kagawa joined the Bank of Tokyo, Ltd. in 1980. He worked primarily in areas related to foreign exchange and treasury, but he was also assigned to the Corporate Planning Office for a period. When the Bank of Tokyo-Mitsubishi UFJ (BTMU) was established in 2006, he was appointed to the position of General Manager of the International Treasury and Investment Division. Over the years, Mr. Kagawa was assigned to several posts related to global markets, such as General Manager of the Global Markets Sales and Trading Division and General Manager of the Financial Markets Division, developing deep expertise in this field. In May 2010, he became an Executive Officer of BTMU and General Manager of the Corporate Risk Management Division, and was also assigned a concurrent position as Executive Manager of the Corporate Risk Management Division at Mitsubishi UFJ Financial Group (MUFG). In 2012, he became a Managing Director, Chief Risk Officer, and Chief Compliance Officer.

Mikio Kajikawa joined the Ministry of Finance in 1982. Since then, he has held a range of important positions mainly in the field of international finance and fiscal policy. His international experience includes the Permanent Delegation to the OECD and as Finance Minister of the Embassy of Japan in Washington, DC, as well as Japan's representative in a number of international meetings related to the Group of Twenty and the Federal Reserve Board. He was Deputy Vice Minister of Finance for International Affairs from 2012 to 2013, and now serves as Senior Deputy Director-General of the International Bureau. He holds a BA in law from the University of Tokyo and an MPA from Princeton University.

Masahiro Kawai was appointed Dean and CEO of the Asian Development Bank Institute in January 2007. He was previously special advisor to the ADB President in charge of regional economic cooperation and integration. Before that, he was an associate professor of economics at Johns Hopkins University and then a professor of economics at the University of Tokyo. He also served as Chief Economist for the World Bank's East Asia and the Pacific Region and as Deputy Vice Minister for International Affairs of Japan's Ministry of Finance. His recent publications focus on economic regionalism. He holds a BA in economics from the University of Tokyo and a PhD in economics from Stanford University.

Peter Morgan is Senior Consultant for Research, Asian Development Bank Institute. He joined the ADBI in December 2008. Previously, he served in Hong Kong, China as Chief Asia Economist for HSBC, responsible for macroeconomic analysis and forecasting for Asia. Before that, he was Chief Japan Economist for HSBC, and earlier held similar positions at Merrill Lynch, Barclays de Zoete Wedd, and Jardine Fleming. Prior to entering the financial industry, he worked as a consultant for Meta Systems Inc. in Cambridge, Massachusetts in the United States, specializing in energy and environmental areas, including energy policy issues in Asian countries, and at International Business Information KK in Tokyo, specializing in financial sector consulting. His research areas are macroeconomic policy and financial sector regulation and reform. Recent publications include *Regional and Global Monetary Cooperation* and *The Role of Macroeconomic Policy in Rebalancing Growth*. He co-edited the volumes *Implications of the Global Financial Crisis for Financial Reform and Regulation in Asia* and *Monetary and Currency Policy Management in Asia*. He earned his MA and PhD degrees in economics from Yale University.

Tokio Morita joined the Ministry of Finance in 1985 and was in charge of enacting and revising elements of the legal framework of Japanese financial system, including the Deposit Insurance Law, the Financial System Restructuring Law, and the Act on the Sales of Financial Products. He worked as Assistant to the Executive Director for Japan at the IMF and also as Advisor in the Monetary and Capital Markets Department, IMF. In July 2007, he was appointed Director of Securities Business Division and then Director of Banks Division I at the Financial Services Agency, Japan. In addition, from November 2007 to September 2009, he served as Chairperson of IOSCO's Standing Committee 3, which is in charge of issues related to investment banks and broker-dealers regulation and supervision. He now serves as Deputy Commissioner for International Affairs, FSA.

Yoshiaki Ogura is Associate Professor at the School of Political Science and Economics (SPSE), Waseda University. He received his PhD in economics from Columbia University in 2005. Before joining SPSE at Waseda University in 2012, he gained experience in academic research and teaching as a research fellow at the Center for Advanced Policy Studies, Kyoto Institute of Economic Research, Kyoto University; as an assistant professor at the Institute of Economic Research, Hitotsubashi University; and as an associate professor at the Faculty of Business Administration, Ritsumeikan University. His main research area is banking. His recent publications in academic journals include "Lending Competition and Credit Availability for New Firms: Empirical Study with the Price Cost Margin in Regional Loan Markets" (*Journal of Banking & Finance,* 2012) and "Interbank Competition and Information Acquisition: Evidence from the Interest Rate Difference" (*Journal of Financial Intermediation,* 2010).

Hiroshi Okada has been a member of the House of Councillors since 2003. Before he was elected to the House of Councillors, he served two terms in the Ibaraki Prefectural Assembly for 7 years and three terms as mayor of Mito City for 10 years. In 2013, he assumed the position as Senior Vice-Minister of Cabinet Office and Senior Vice-Minister for Reconstruction in the second Abe Cabinet. His main responsibility includes financial services affairs and revitalization of businesses damaged by the Great East Japan Earthquake. He is also in charge of food safety policies, convivial society policies, gender equality policies, and consumer policies. He has a bachelor's degree in social sciences from Ritsumeikan University.

Hisashi Ono joined the Ministry of Finance in 1983. He has extensive experience both at home and abroad. He worked at other agencies in Japan such as the National Tax Agency and the Economic Planning Agency. His international experience includes being Assistant to the Executive Director for Japan at the Inter-American Development Bank and Senior Executive Advisor to the President of the Asian Development Bank. Further, at the time when he was Director of Regional Financial Cooperation Division, International Bureau at the Ministry of Finance, he was in charge of the Chiang Mai Initiative. At the Financial Services Agency, Japan (FSA), he served in various positions including Director of the Research Office, Inspection Bureau, Director of the Insurance Business Division, Supervisory Bureau, and he served as Director for the Credit System, Director of the Planning Division, and Deputy Director General in the Planning and Coordination Bureau before assuming his current position in 2012. Currently, he also serves as Deputy Director General of the Reconstruction Agency and as Director in charge of the Regional Economy Vitalization Corporation of Japan (REVIC) at the Cabinet Office. He received his bachelor's degree from the College of Arts and Sciences of the University of Tokyo.

Jae-Ha Park is ADBI's Deputy Dean for Special Activities. He was previously Vice President of the Korea Institute of Finance. He worked for numerous public positions in the Republic of Korea, such as Senior Advisor to the Minister of Finance and Economy and Director General of the Task Force for Economic Restructuring in the Office of the President. He has also served as Chairman of the Board of Directors of Shinhan Bank, which is the largest commercial bank in the Republic of Korea. His recent areas of interest are regional economic and financial cooperation, and financial market development in Asia. He holds a BA in economics from Seoul National University and a PhD in economics from Pennsylvania State University.

Julius Caesar Parreñas is Advisor on International Affairs of Bank of Tokyo-Mitsubishi UFJ and Senior Advisory Fellow at the Institute for International Monetary Affairs in Tokyo. He is also coordinator of the Advisory Group on APEC Financial System Capacity Building, the Asia-Pacific Financial Forum (APFF), and the Asia-Pacific Infrastructure Partnership (APIP). He served in the past as Senior Advisor to the Chairman of Chinatrust Financial Holding and several Asian financial institutions. He was Policy Advocacy Committee Coordinator of the Asian Bankers' Association and an alternate member of the APEC Business Advisory Council (ABAC). He was Executive Director of ABAC in 1996–1997, while concurrently serving as Executive Director of the Center for Research and Communication and Professor at the School of Economics of the University of Asia and the Pacific. From 1994 to 1998, he was an advisor on World Trade Organization and Association of Southeast Asian Nations Free Trade Area affairs under the Office of the President of the Republic of the Philippines. He also served as consultant to the Philippine Senate, various international agencies, and major private corporations in the world. He received his PhD, *magna cum laude,* from Ludwig Maximilian University in Munich, Federal Republic of Germany, in 1988. He has authored various books and over 90 articles on international finance, economics, and trade.

Victor Pontines joined ADBI in May 2012. He specializes in the broad areas of open-economy macroeconomics and international finance with particular reference to the East Asian region. He has published widely as book chapters and in scholarly journals. Before joining ADBI, he was seconded by Bank Negara Malaysia as Senior Economist for The South East Asian Central Banks (SEACEN) Research and Training Centre in Kuala Lumpur, Malaysia. Previous to this, he taught at Flinders Business School, Flinders University in Australia; School of Economics at the University of Adelaide in Australia and at the Australia branch of the Heinz School of Public Policy and Management of Carnegie Mellon University. He started as a lecturer in the Department of Economics, De La Salle University in the Philippines and has worked for the Department of Economic Research of the Bangko Sentral ng Pilipinas (Central Bank of the Philippines). He holds economics degrees from De La Salle University (BA, MSc) in the Philippines, University of Exeter (MA with distinction) in the UK, and from the University of Adelaide (PhD) in Australia.

Ratna Sahay is Deputy Director (Strategy, Planning, and Coordination) of the Monetary and Capital Markets Department at the IMF. She is responsible for setting strategic priorities for the department, developing policy positions, ensuring quality control, and coordinating the work and resource management of the department. She led the paper on setting a medium-term financial surveillance strategy for the IMF last year. She has worked in the Asian, European, Middle East, and Western Hemisphere Department, leading several missions to emerging market countries. She has led or contributed to key analytical and policy initiatives in the Research, Monetary and Capital Markets, and Finance Departments. In her previous roles, she has served as Advisor to Stanley Fischer (First Deputy Managing Director) and Michael Mussa and Kenneth Rogoff (both Economic Counselors of the IMF). She has led regional surveillance in the Middle East and Western Hemisphere Departments, coordinated IMF-wide research on low-income countries, and led an international effort on raising funds for clearing Liberia's debt arrears and providing debt relief. She has published widely in leading journals on financial market spillovers and financial crises, economic growth, fiscal policy and debt sustainability, and transition economies. She has taught at Delhi University, Columbia University, and New York University and holds a PhD in economics from New York University.

Jongsoon Shin is an Economist in the Regional Office for Asia and the Pacific in the IMF's Asia and Pacific Department. Mr. Shin joined in the Japan Financial Sector Assessment Program (FSAP) mission, Mongolia Article IV missions, and Global Financial Stability Report (GFSR) missions. His publications include "What Role Can Financial Policies Play in Revitalizing SMEs in Japan?" (co-authored, WP 12/291, Dec 2012) and "Japan FSAP Technical Note: Credit Intermediation" (co-authored, Sep 2012). He also contributed to the 2013 Spillover Report and the Global Financial Stability Report (Apr 2013). Prior to the IMF, he worked for the Ministry of Finance and Economy (Macroeconomic Team, and Tax Office) as well as for the Financial Services Commission (Banking Division) of the Republic of Korea. He also worked at the United States Department of the Interior. He holds an MBA in finance from the Wharton School of the University of Pennsylvania, and earned his BA from Seoul National University.

Suhaedi After he joined Bank Indonesia in 1988, Suhaedi spent the majority of his career in the Directorate of Economic Research and Monetary Policy (DKM). His international experience has been influenced by his position as Economist in Bank Indonesia's representative office in Tokyo. He also had a chance to broaden his knowledge when he was positioned as Visiting Researcher at the Ministry of Finance. In 2008, he spent some time as the Head of the External Relation Team until he was promoted to Advisor at the Directorate of Banking Research and Regulation and became in charge of the process of the Indonesian Financial Sector Assessment Program (FSAP). In 2012, he was assigned as Director of Bank Indonesia Regional North Sulawesi Province and in 2013 promoted to Executive Director at Bank Indonesia Regional Office for Eastern Indonesia. His main duty is achieving price stability through synergetic actions with local authorities, supervising bank and payment system, and promoting financial inclusion. He initiated a new approach to promote access to finance through active involvement of religious leaders and institutions. The rationale and implementation of this approach was presented at the Asia-Pacific Economic Cooperation Workshop on Financial Inclusion in May 2013. He received his bachelor's degree from Bandung Institute of Technology Indonesia in 1986 and a master's degree in public policy from Saitama University (GRIPS), Japan.

Salinee Wangtal is an Assistant Governor of the Supervision Group at the Bank of Thailand. Her duties in supervising and examining Thai financial institutions rely mainly on the micro prudential approach, which focuses on proper risk management and good governance within financial institutions led to overall financial system stability. She has vast experience in financial sector development and regulation, including crisis management and resolution framework. During the Asian financial crisis in 1997–1999, she was involved in the resolution and restructuring process of several failed financial institutions. In addition, she also introduced the international supervision standard to the Thai banking system. Mrs. Salinee also served as a Managing Director at Nakhonthon Bank (PLC) in 1999 and as a Deputy Managing Director at Thai Military Bank (PLC) (TMB Bank) from 2001–2002. She is currently serving on several government affairs committees, such as Secretary of the Committee for the Protection of Credit Information, Director of the Deposit Protection Agency Board, the Regulatory Commission on Accounting Profession for the Accounting Profession Act of 2004, the Comparative Joint Committee for the Financial Institution Act of 2008, and the Comparative Joint Committee for the Provident Fund Act of 1987 and Securities and Exchange Act of 1992.

Wako Watanabe is Professor of Economics at the Faculty of Business and Commerce, Keio University. He worked previously at the Ministry of International Affairs and Communications, Osaka University, and Tohoku University. His area of expertise is empirical research of the banking sector, with a special emphasis on regulations and government involvement in the sector. He received his PhD in economics from Princeton University. His recent publications in academic journals include "Prudential Regulation and the 'Credit Crunch': Evidence from Japan" (*Journal of Money, Credit and Banking,* 2007) and "Does a Large Loss of Bank Capital Cause Evergreening? Evidence from Japan" (*Journal of the Japanese and International Economies,* 2010).

Tarisa Watanagase joined the Bank of Thailand in 1975 and was Governor between 2006 and 2010. Her long career at the Bank of Thailand included responsibilities in economic research, money market operation, payment systems, banking sector policy and supervision, and monetary policy. She also worked as an economist at the IMF in Washington, DC between 1988 and 1990 and as an IMF–World Bank FSAP independent assessor in 2002. She was instrumental in the 1997 Thai crisis resolution and the ensuing supervisory and financial sector reforms, the establishment of the Thai Real-Time-Gross-Settlement (RTGS) system in 1995, the first in Asia, to eliminate settlement risk in high-value fund transfers, and in influencing the law makers for the passage of the new Bank of Thailand Act in 2008, which guarantees the bank's independence. Currently, she speaks extensively on central banking and financial sector issues and is a board member or advisor to several public and private organizations, both domestic and international.

Pungky P. Wibowo is currently Director of the Financial Access and SME Development Department of Bank Indonesia (Central Bank of Indonesia). He is also team leader for the financial inclusion framework strategy for Indonesia, team leader for the national campaign for financial education conducted by Bank Indonesia, and team leader on the task force for development of branchless banking in Indonesia. He is an active member of the Alliance on Financial Inclusion (AFI), the Organisation for Economic Co-operation and Development (OECD)/International Network on Financial Education (INFE), and G20 Global Partnership on Financial Inclusion (GPFI). From 2010–2013, he was Deputy Director of the Financial System Stability Group of the Banking Research and Regulation Department. He received his PhD in money, banking, and finance from the University of Birmingham, London and an MSc from the University of Wollonggong, Australia in banking portfolio behavior.

Ganeshan Wignaraja is Director of Research at the Asian Development Bank Institute in Tokyo. His main research interests are in trade and competitiveness, regional integration, macroeconomic forecasting, technology, and foreign aid. He has published 12 books in these areas (including *Asia's Free Trade Agreements* and *Competitiveness Strategies in Developing Countries*) and is an Executive Editor of the *Journal of Asian Economics*. Formerly, he was Principal Economist in the Asian Development Bank's Office of Regional Economic Integration, Chief Programme Officer in the Commonwealth Secretariat, and a manager in a leading United Kingdom economics consulting firm. He has also held research positions at Oxford University, the Organisation for Economic Co-operation and Development, and the United Nations University Institute for New Technologies. His doctorate in economics is from Oxford University.

Naoyuki Yoshino is Dean and CEO of the Asian Development Institute in Tokyo. He obtained his PhD from Johns Hopkins University in 1979. He was a visiting scholar at the Massachusetts Institute of Technology and has been a visiting professor at New South Wales University (Australia), Institute d'Etudes politiques de Paris (Paris), and Gothenburg University (Sweden). He was an assistant professor at the State University of New York at Buffalo before he joined Keio University in 1991. His professional career includes membership in government committees. He was appointed as Chair of the Financial Planning Standard Board (FPSB) in 2007. Since 2004, he has been a Director of the Financial Research Center (FSA Institute), Japan. In recognition of his wide-ranging scholarship and contribution to policy formulation, he was conferred an honorary doctorate by Gothenburg University in Sweden in 2004 and Martin-Luther-University Halle-Wittenberg in Germany in 2013. He was included in the "Who's Who in the World" list in 2009 and 2010. He received the World Top 100 Educators' Award in 2009 in Cambridge, UK. His publications include *Postal Saving and Fiscal Investment in Japan* (Oxford University Press) and *Hometown Investment Trust Funds—A Stable Way to Supply Risk Capital* (Springer).

Abbreviations

ADB	Asian Development Bank
ADBI	Asian Development Bank Institute
ASEAN	Association of Southeast Asian Nations
BIS	Bank for International Settlements
CRD	Credit Risk Database
FSA	Financial Services Agency
FSB	Financial Stability Board
G20	Group of Twenty
GDP	gross domestic product
GFC	Global Financial Crisis
G-SIFI	global systemically important financial institution
ICT	information and communication technology
IFC	International Finance Corporation
IMF	International Monetary Fund
JGB	Japanese government bond
NISA	Nippon Individual Savings Account
NPL	nonperforming loan
OECD	Organisation for Economic Co-operation and Development
PRC	People's Republic of China
SIFI	systemically important financial institution
SMEs	small and medium-sized enterprises
TBTF	too big to fail
UK	United Kingdom
US	United States

Welcoming Remarks

Hiroshi Okada

At the outset of the International Conference "Financial System Stability, Regulation, and Financial Inclusion," organized jointly by the Financial Services Agency (FSA) of Japan, the Asian Development Bank Institute (ADBI), and the International Monetary Fund (IMF), allow me to say a few words.

First of all, on behalf of the FSA of Japan, I would like to thank Dr. Muliaman D. Hadad, Chairman of the Financial Services Authority, Indonesia; Dr. Tarisa Watanagase, Former Governor, Bank of Thailand; Dr. Ranee Jayamaha, Former Deputy Governor of the Central Bank of Sri Lanka; and other speakers, panelists, and our participants. Welcome. Also, I take this opportunity to thank those at ADBI and IMF who have helped us in jointly hosting this conference. Thank you so much.

Under the theme of Financial System Stability, Regulation, and Financial Inclusion, we will discuss the way financial supervision should be conducted to maintain financial system stability and to promote competition in the financial sector; challenges in small and medium-sized enterprise (SME) finance and financial inclusion in Asia; and financial systems desirable for Asian economic growth. The topics are very timely and I personally look forward to the outcome of the discussions today.

If I were to draw an analogy: money is like blood in the human body, and without blood the body is no longer viable. Without a smooth money flow, economic activities cannot be viable. In that regard, the role of finance, which facilitates the money flow, is of critical importance the world over. Different countries face different policy challenges. For Japan, the biggest challenge at the moment is to end prolonged deflation and to revive the economy. The administration of Prime Minister Abe is addressing the challenge by use of its "three arrows," namely bold monetary policy, flexible fiscal policy, and a growth strategy to stimulate private investments.

How to assist these initiatives in terms of the financial aspect is of great importance. Japan's strength lies in design and manufacturing. In order to financially

H. Okada
Cabinet Office for Financial Services, Tokyo, Japan

ADB Institute, Financial Services Agency, Japan, International Monetary Fund Regional Office for Asia and the Pacific (eds.), *Financial System Stability, Regulation, and Financial Inclusion,* ADB Institute Series on Development Economics, DOI 10.1007/978-4-431-55254-3_1

enhance their strength, we need to strengthen financial services' functions, so that both financial services and the real economy can grow as two wheels of a cart. The Expert Panel, which was established in 2013, put together a set of measures at the end of last December to revitalize financial and capital markets to achieve the goal of realizing Tokyo's status as an international financial center by 2020 when Tokyo will be hosting the Olympic Games.

One of the measures in the Expert Panel's recommendation is the utilization of a major financial potential in Japan, namely the utilization of its 1600 trillion yen worth of household financial assets. Most of the household financial assets are deposits. If even only a part of this could be utilized by companies with promising technologies, we could commercialize such technologies, which in turn could revitalize the economy. In order to mobilize household financial assets in closed areas, the FSA of Japan introduced the Nippon Individual Savings Account (NISA) at the beginning of 2014.

In December 2013, a working group under the Financial System Council compiled a report on their discussion to enhance cloud funding as a tool to provide necessary funding at the time of commercializing technologies and ideas. We are now working on the institutional design based on these recommendations.

Initiatives such as NISA, a Japanese version of the personal savings account, could broaden the base of retail investors. And financial education, a theme of this conference, is a critical element. Finance is relevant for everyone in a modern society, not just for those who are investing for the first time. Enhanced financial literacy will protect investors from troubles related to financial transactions, and by using financial products wisely, quality of life could improve.

If we can produce competent investors through financial and economic education, the markets will be revitalized and that in itself could be a new potential for the Japanese economy. The FSA of Japan believes in the importance of financial literacy for all, and it is promoting financial and economic education in partnerships with other government ministries, agencies, and relevant organizations.

For SMEs, financial institutions must further enhance their financial intermediary functions to promote turnaround and growth of companies and to revitalize the local economy. The financial institutions' active involvement in business improvement of client companies, not just by providing financing, allows both business entities and financial institutions to grow, which in turn will lead to the growth of the economy as a whole. That is why the FSA of Japan has been encouraging financial institutions to actively provide funding, including new loans to SMEs, and to engage in improving clients' businesses and financial strength.

During a later session today, there will be a detailed presentation of Japan's experience in that area by an FSA official in charge. More recently, both Japanese companies and financial institutions have been increasingly active in other Asian countries and we see stronger economic ties with those countries in Asia. The FSA of Japan is actively helping in developing financial infrastructure in Asia, moving to build a virtuous cycle, a positive cycle of us contributing to the Asian economic development and facilitating the growth of Japanese companies, which should benefit from growth in Asia.

Through these initiatives, we are committed to do our utmost in terms of the financial aspects, to put an end to deflation and to realize sustainable economic growth in Japan. Needless to say, financial stability is of the utmost importance. The FSA has been actively engaged in the discussion to prevent the recurrence of financial crises and to achieve financial stability in such forums as the Group of Twenty (G20) Summit.

In June 2013, the FSA established a framework for orderly resolution of financial institutions to ensure financial stability even in the wake of a market-based financial crisis such as the one we saw some years ago. At present, the Japanese financial system is on the whole sound and stable. In order to contribute to global financial stability, we are committed to steadily supporting the financial systems.

Japan has a track record as an international financial center. We have learned from the history of financial services in Japan and Japan has participated in discussions on financial regulatory reforms in international conferences. Based on such experiences, Japan aims to develop financial and capital markets in Asia together with all of you in Asia. I know there are many participants who are from Asian countries.

Japan continues to place the utmost importance on our ties with our neighbors, such as the People's Republic of China (PRC) and the Republic of Korea, and with Association of Southeast Asian Nations (ASEAN) member states such as Thailand and Indonesia, and with countries that are connected by sea, like India. In the financial field in particular, we want to enhance our collaboration through supporting developments of both legal frameworks and on the intangible infrastructure and settlement system and other tangible infrastructure and through sharing knowledge and experiences on tools to manage financial administration.

Against this backdrop, it is truly meaningful that there will be active discussion among experts from around the world, including Asia, on the theme of Financial System Stability, Regulation, and Financial Inclusion.

I hope this conference will be conducive in further developing financial and capital markets in Asia, and with that I would like to conclude my opening remarks. Thank you very much for your attention.

Session 1: Financial System Stability and Competition in the Financial Industry

Odd Per Brekk, Ratna Sahay, Akira Ariyoshi, Tokio Morita, Akihiko Kagawa, and Jae-Ha Park

Address by Session Chair

Odd Per Brekk

Good morning everybody, and before we start, allow me on behalf of the IMF's Regional Office for Asia and the Pacific to thank both ADBI and the FSA for co-hosting this event with us, and of course all of you for participating and coming here to contribute and participate this morning. We look forward to an interesting day of discussions on a range of financial sector issues, all of which are at the center of the international policy debate today.

The first panel of the conference will focus on stability and competition in the financial industry. To set the stage for the discussions, let us remind ourselves a bit about the broader backdrop for this. First of all, it may be useful to keep in mind through all of the detailed discussions that we will have, that the basic objective of what we are discussing is to achieve stable, long-term economic growth.

In this regard, we know that banks provide important support to a country's economy by transforming savings into productive investment. At the same time, we also know

O. P. Brekk
Regional Office for Asia and the Pacific, International Monetary Fund, Tokyo, Japan

R. Sahay
Monetary and Capital Markets Department, International Monetary Fund, Washington, DC, USA

A. Ariyoshi
School of International and Public Policy, Hitotsubashi University, Tokyo, Japan

T. Morita
Financial Services Agency, Tokyo, Japan

A. Kagawa
Mitsubishi UFJ Financial Group, Inc., Tokyo, Japan

J.-H. Park
Asian Development Bank Institute, Tokyo, Japan

ADB Institute, Financial Services Agency, Japan, International Monetary Fund Regional Office for Asia and the Pacific (eds.), *Financial System Stability, Regulation, and Financial Inclusion,* ADB Institute Series on Development Economics, DOI 10.1007/978-4-431-55254-3_2

that maturity transformation makes banks inherently fragile, that the often opaque interconnectedness between financial institutions makes the sector prone to panics and runs, and also that the "too-big-to-fail" issue tends to exacerbate moral hazard.

So this means that we will be facing trade-offs when we think about policies. On the one hand, high growth may be helped by a competitive and highly developed financial sector, through better mobilization of resources, and better and more efficient allocation of these resources. On the other hand, a more developed financial sector might carry larger stability risks.

What are the policy implications of this? Looking back at the onset of the Global Financial Crisis, a failure of regulation was clearly a major factor in 2008. This is of course a common view and the international community's effort in the subsequent years has focused on policies to bolster stability.

With these considerations in mind, a number of issues arise. Where do we stand on the regulatory reform agenda? What should be the role of competition policies versus regulation? Has the focus on stability come at the cost of growth and recovery? And what are the key steps and priorities going forward?

To make sense of these issues, we are lucky to have a very distinguished group of speakers on this panel who together bring to the discussion a diverse set of perspectives as academics, as policymakers, and also as practitioners.

Financial System Stability and Competition: Do They Complement or Clash?

Ratna Sahay[1]

Motivation

Thank you very much for inviting me to speak at this conference; it is certainly a timely topic, especially since the issues are complex and the answers not straightforward. The Global Financial Crisis (GFC) has squarely put financial stability at the center stage. Since then, national and international policymakers have been preoccupied with managing the crisis and designing regulatory reforms to stem future systemic risk.

Not surprisingly, the focus, so far, has been on restoring and enhancing financial stability, with limited discussion on whether more needs to be done to secure competition and ensure access to finance. At the same time, since the GFC, the number of financial institutions has fallen across the globe, even as their total assets have increased and the derivatives market is now 10 times gross domestic product (GDP) (Figs. 1 and 2).

[1] The views expressed in this presentation are those of the author and should not be reported as or attributed to the International Monetary Fund, its Executive Board, or the governments of any of its members.

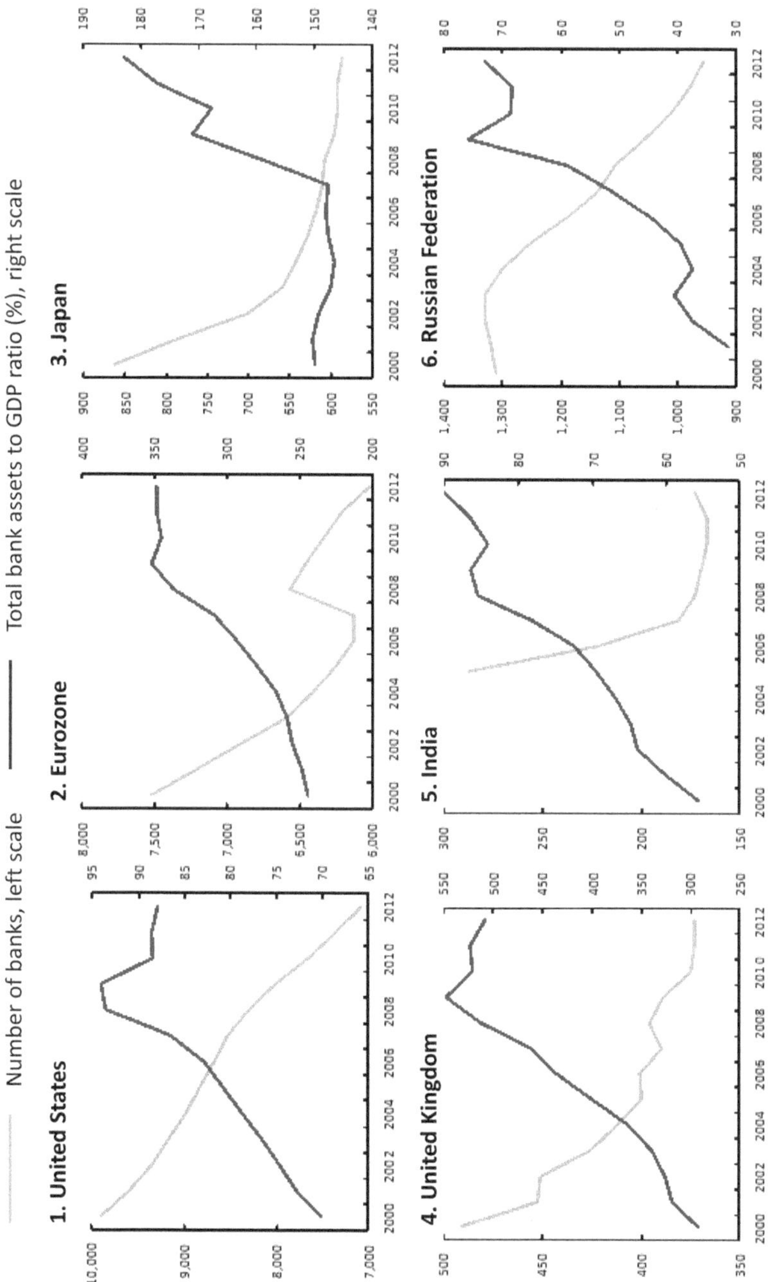

Fig. 1 Number and size of banks in selected economies. *GDP* gross domestic product. (Source: IMF 2013a)

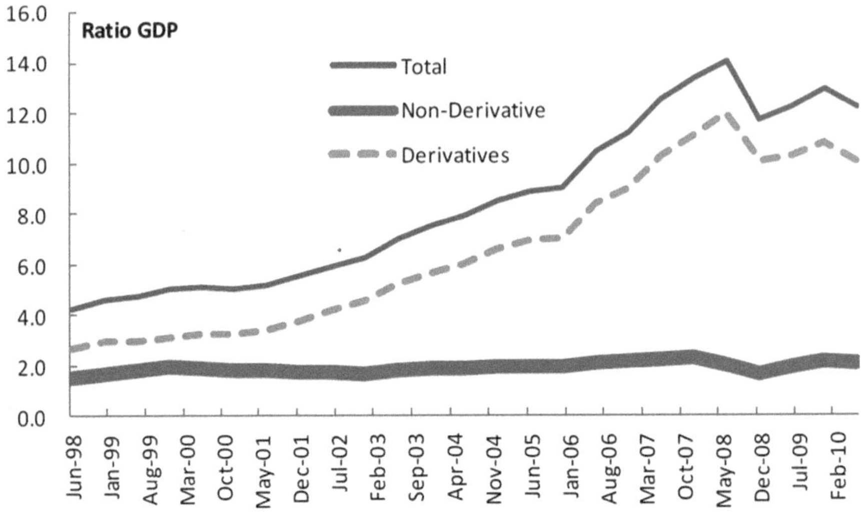

Fig. 2 Global notional derivatives versus primary securities. *GDP* gross domestic product. (Source: OECD 2011, Chap. 2)

Against this background, two key policy questions arise:

- Are we doing enough to ensure global and national financial stability so that we are better prepared for future crises?
- Are there unintended consequences of the ongoing reforms on the incentives for entry of new financial firms? In other words, would competition in the financial sector and access to finance become collateral damage in our battle against systemic risk?

Evidence

At this stage, the reforms are still ongoing and the consequences, both intended and unintended, will naturally evolve with time. But we have accumulated sufficient experience across countries in the last two decades to draw three inferences:

- First, competition is good for access to finance.
- Second, the evidence that competition undermines financial stability remains elusive.
- And third, the GFC revealed major fault lines in the intermediation structure, notably the too-big-to-fail problem.

Competition

It is well accepted that greater competition in financial services improves efficiency and productivity, by lowering the cost of borrowing, improving access to finance, and enhancing the availability and quality of financial services and products through innovation. Investment banking and nonbank financial intermediation have increased market depth and broadened access to finance in advanced economies. Cross-border banking has deepened markets in emerging economies. There is also evidence that it has a positive effect on economic growth—for example, Claessens and Laeven (2005) found that industrial growth increases with increasing competition in 16 banking systems (see also World Bank 2013).

Competition authorities use various tools to enhance competition in the financial sector: lowering entry barriers, allowing more banks including foreign bank branches, making markets and products more contestable (such as through credit registries in retail banking), eliminating activity restrictions, and introducing or enhancing new lending markets such as commercial paper or the corporate bond market.

Of course, the process of financial deepening and innovation can bring with it risks that are not fully internalized by financial institutions as the GFC crisis revealed; regulation and supervision were too lax and incentives for adequate risk management were missing. Still, the positive aspects of the deregulation and the expansion in market-based financial intermediation of the past two decades should not be underestimated.

Link between Competition and Financial Stability

Unfortunately, the empirical and theoretical literature has been ambiguous in its findings and predictions on whether competition is good or bad for financial stability (Claessens 2009; OECD 2011). One concern is the effect of higher competition on banks' incentives for risk-taking and their franchise values. Excessive competition, as one side of the argument goes, can lead to greater fragility and instability as banks take on more risk by competing for market shares. This can lead to weaker lending standards even as access to finance tends to increase during good times.

Thus, we see how potential tensions between competition policy and financial stability policy can arise. For instance, if there was indeed evidence to support that a larger number of banks lead to more risk-taking by the banks, then restraints on entry and encouraging larger players would be viewed as necessary to preserve financial stability (IMF 2013b). But, such policies could incentivize banks to reap economies of scope and scale by becoming even bigger, expanding across product lines and national borders. This, as we well know, reinforced the too-big-to-fail problem that was at the heart of the recent crisis.

The empirical literature has not found decisive links between various measures of competition and financial stability. For instance, our 2012 Global Financial Stability Report found that higher concentration in the banking sector was associated with higher GDP growth in good times, but higher financial stress during a banking crisis (IMF 2012a). At the same time, banking systems with high concentration ratios had very different experiences during the GFC—Ireland and Iceland had severe banking crises, whereas Canada and Australia did not. Of course, measures of concentration may not be related to competition per se. A key message from the crisis is that what matters more than the structure of the market itself is making sure that there is a robust regulatory and supervisory framework.

Fault Lines

It is now well accepted that financial systems and instruments became highly complex and the location of risks was opaque, especially for over-the-counter derivatives and other securitization products. This made it difficult for both authorities and investors to track risks and assess potential spillovers, and to understand the underlying elements of new financial instruments (IMF 2012b). Assessment of risks by credit rating agencies, on which the official and private sector rely heavily for critical decisions, also became suspect. Aided by technological advances, financial institutions became more interconnected through interbank, repo, and other wholesale markets, both domestically and globally. The upshot of these developments was the evolution of large and complex institutions, performing a wide range of financial services across international borders and offering products that are often opaque.

When the crisis came, it became evident that to maintain financial stability, these large institutions—the systemically important financial institutions (SIFIs) and the global SIFIS (G-SIFIs)—were too important to go bust. Public intervention in various forms had created the implicit expectation of future support. This had created a "too-big-or-too-important-to-fail" (henceforth, TBTF) subsidy, with large banks benefitting more from this than smaller banks (Noss and Sowerbutts 2012). The forthcoming Global Financial Stability Report (GFSR) provides estimates of the value of this subsidy. The subsidy gives rise to unfair competition in the funding markets, and encourages TBTFs to become even bigger.

TBTF: Are Current Reforms Sufficient?

Let me now turn to answering the questions that I started with—are we doing enough to ensure financial stability, especially on the TBTF concern, and do the reforms have unintended consequences for competition? In particular, the big question is whether the enhanced capital and liquidity requirements provide disincentives for new entrants in the intermediation landscape, or provide disincentives to banks to become larger and more complex, which should help competition.

A host of reforms are aimed at addressing the systemic risk systemically important financial institutions pose. As a first step, the reforms involve identification of SIFIs. In this regard, the IMF, together with the Financial Stability Board (FSB) and the Bank for International Settlements (BIS), came up with a methodology to identify the SIFIs (IMF et al. 2009). The shared characteristics of SIFIs were size, complexity, and opaqueness, with operations difficult to substitute and replace in the event of crisis, and interconnectedness with other financial institutions. The idea of substitutability is related to the entry of new firms, that is, competition.

While dealing with the GFC did exacerbate the problems associated with the SIFIs, some progress has been made on global regulatory reforms, namely in imposing higher regulatory capital and liquidity requirements on SIFIs through Basel III, requiring greater supervisory intensity, introducing bail-in resolutions, and allowing for cross border resolutions. Full implementation, which is pending in the resolutions area, of these bank reforms should help address market distortions manifested by underpricing of risk.

Establishing a SIFI framework for non-banks has been a slower process due to differences in business models and the heterogeneity of the nonbank sector.

As banks shed costly activities (for instance, the trading and investment portfolios lines as some banks have done), the risk is that either they will move over to non-banks or they will further concentrate this activity towards ones with an already high share of such business. The shift in activities to non-banks and shadow banks could be good for competition as long as the risks are monitored and adequately addressed through intensive supervision.

Structural constraints on banks' activities in three jurisdictions have been designed to separate trading activities from the more traditional deposit taking activities, as the former are riskier. The Volcker Rule prohibits United States (US) banks' proprietary trading, and the Vickers and Liikanen proposals in the United Kingdom (UK) and the eurozone, respectively, segregate a wide range of non-core activities into ring-fenced activities. Once core and non-core activities are separated, other policies such as competition policy could be used to deal with entry/exit of firms targeting a market segment.

These structural measures, particularly in tandem with other regulatory reforms (such as higher capital requirements) could mitigate excessive risk taking by the SIFIs. However, they also have implications for lower diversification benefits and efficiency, making the financial sector as a whole less profitable and efficient. Also, to the extent that these reforms are not global, it would be an uneven playing field for these banks competing against local banks in other jurisdictions. This points to the need for a global cost-benefit exercise encompassing extra-territorial implications of structural measures (Viñals et al. 2013). This is a big unknown.

Would these reforms, including loss-absorbing capacities and resolvability of SIFIs, be enough to solve the TBTF problem and promote a competitive landscape? I am afraid we have some ways to go before we can say that. I will point to five other areas that need more work to adequately address the TBTF problem:

- Supervision—providing sufficient resources and independence to supervisors needs to match the stronger and stricter regulatory rules (Viñals and Fiechter 2010).
- Shadow Banks—regulatory standards for banks' interaction with shadow banks are being tightened but national implementation is pending.
- Credit Rating Agencies—reducing mechanistic regulatory reliance on CRAs.
- Accounting standards—harmonizing audit standards, which vary across and within jurisdictions.
- Derivatives reform—more progress in dealing with the problems created by the leverage and opaqueness of derivatives revealed during the GFC.

Where Should Competition Policy Head?

Let me now raise the question of whether competition policy could play a more prominent role in addressing the TBTF problem. The argument is that anti-trust actions, such as preventing mergers between banks or breaking up large institutions, or downsizing them by selling part of their businesses, could avoid moral hazards associated with the creation of too large and complex and systemically important institutions. This is an area of growing interest and research (Ratnovski 2013). In some countries, such as recently in the US, the traditional powers of competition policy, including licensing, take-over control, and break-up powers, have been vested on the prudential authorities to improve the resolvability of systemically important institutions.

At the very least, strong coordination and consultation mechanisms would need to exist between the prudential and competitive authorities (IMF 2013b).

Finally, let me move on to the question of whether the regulatory reforms would excessively undermine access to finance. This concern has widely been expressed by, in particular, developing and emerging economies, but is also valid in advanced economies, for example with regard to SMEs. The new capital and liquidity regulations may lower banks' ability to provide long-term financing for investment, including in infrastructure (FSB 2013). Furthermore, less financial hedging and more risk-retention due to stricter derivatives regulations could also impede long-term financing of projects.

While these are valid concerns, the most important contribution of financial regulation to long-term investment finance is to promote a safe, sound, and resilient financial system. Furthermore, alternative solutions could be explored to diversify the financial system and enhance the functioning of capital markets as sources of long-term financing. This can include further deepening the local equity and corporate debt markets, developing securitized markets and the local institutional investor base, as well as addressing gaps in market infrastructure that may be impeding these markets from taking off. The associated financial stability risks could be contained through appropriate sequencing of reforms and upgrading and strengthening the financial sector regulatory and supervisory frameworks.

Conclusion

Let me conclude by making three points. First, there is no doubt that financial innovation has been a powerful force for improving access and reducing the cost of finance and broadening access to new financial products. However, to reap the full benefits from competition, regulations and supervision need to be strengthened accordingly to capture potential new risks caught up with these developments. Competition policies can play a much greater role in enhancing both market efficiency and innovation in the financial sector once we have strong regulations and intensive supervision in place. Prudential and competition authorities need to closely coordinate with each other, especially in dealing with the TBTF problem or to help facilitate crisis resolution.

Second, there is a need to address the risks in the nonbank and shadow banking sectors as activity is expected to shift here from banks. We could miss the opportunity for healthy competition between banks and non-banks, including shadow banks, due to inconsistent application of regulatory standards between bank and nonbank SIFIs.

Third, there is a case for developing "missing markets" in enhancing access to finance in Emerging Market and Developing Economies (EMDEs) as regulatory reforms are being implemented. Thank you.

Navigating the Financial Regulator's Impossible Trinity

Akira Ariyoshi

Good morning and first let me thank the organizers for giving me an opportunity to speak at this very interesting as well as important event. As time is limited I would like to go immediately into the substance of my talk, but before I do, just let me give one disclaimer. After over 30 years in the public sector, I moved to academia some 4 years ago. A lot of my old friends from the public sector asked me how I feel about it. I have a set answer to that question, and that is that one gets freedom of speech, but the downside is that nobody listens to you. And one tends to end up shouting in order to attract attention. So, please bear with me if my talk sounds rather crude and simplistic compared with the more thoughtful and nuanced presentations of my former colleagues.

Now, when something bad happens, you ask yourself what did we do wrong and what can we do to make sure that these things do not happen again? The major lesson that the regulators have drawn from the last crisis appears to be that there was too little capital, both in terms of preventing the crisis and in terms of avoiding a massive cost of cleanup to the taxpayers. This looks on the surface like a reasonable lesson, as capital adequacy rules have indeed been the central pillar of prudential regulation. So if a lot of banks go bust at the same time, that is a prima facie evidence that capital was indeed insufficient.

But I have some reservations about coming straight to this conclusion. For me, the most telling comments that show what lay behind the crisis are the following by the regulator and the regulated:

> Those of us who have looked to the self-interest of lending institutions to protect shareholders' equity (myself especially) are in a state of shocked disbelief.
> Then FRB Chairman Alan Greenspan (Congressional testimony, 23 October 2008)

> ...as long as the music is playing, you've got to get up and dance. We're still dancing.
> Citigroup then Chairman Chuck Prince (Financial Times, 9 July 2007)

The comment by Alan Greenspan reflects the regulators' view that, essentially, financial institutions do not want to go bust, so they will manage risk in order to safeguard their solvency.

Chuck Prince's comment by the regulated, on the other hand, shows that if even they do recognize the risk they may not be in a position to do anything about it.

Competition—stronger competition—actually strengthened this sort of short-sightedness. It forces the institutions to be short-sighted because you may well be driven out of the market if you do not in some sense disregard the risk. This shows that there is possibly some profound disconnect between what regulators think and how the regulated behave.

I would like to illustrate what I mean focusing on capital adequacy rules, although I believe this issue is more general.

As Alan Greenspan noted, financial institutions will indeed maintain a certain amount of capital with or without regulation, since they do not want to go bust at the first downturn. The amount of financial capital that financial institutions voluntarily set aside is often called economic capital.

But the regulators have chosen to introduce capital adequacy rules. If we just look at the actual amount of capital the banks have held relative to the regulatory minimum, we can generally see that the amount of capital required by regulators has been well below this economic capital. If this is the case, what is the point of having these seemingly redundant capital rules? The logic was that it was designed as a minimum capital standard, essentially to catch deteriorating banks before they actually go bust. This was thought to be necessary because banks might resort to gambling for resurrection when their conditions deteriorate, since the downside for the shareholder is limited in such cases. In order to prevent such behavior, the imposition of prompt corrective actions by the regulator is linked to the breach of the minimum capital standards.

It is important to recognize that it was possible to agree on the same capital standards globally despite differences in business models and economic and market conditions as well as credit cultures across countries, because the rules set the *minimum* capital level. The level was well below what the banks would voluntarily maintain under normal circumstances, and therefore was not really binding in their everyday operations. At the same time, the regulators allowed the use of internal models, trusting that banks understand their own risk best, and because they believed that it would help reduce distortions that standardized measurement of risk through regulations might bring.

Of course, there was a possibility that the capital would turn out to be insufficient in some cases, but safety nets for small savers and systemic events were put into place, and things like a 99 % confidence interval for value at risk were introduced to limit the frequency of occurrences, and the resulting regulatory system gave one a feeling that this should work.

In reality, it did not turn out that well. Firstly, the capital adequacy numbers as calculated and reported by the banks significantly lag their true state. The idea that you can catch banks on their way down before they go bust was too optimistic, because by the time you realized that something was wrong, the bank was probably deeply insolvent.

More fundamentally, the problem was that the banks and shareholders have no incentive to set aside capital for tail risk, because economic capital does not anticipate extreme events. Banks would not voluntarily set aside capital, say, to prepare for a risk that they think might happen once in 100 years, and competition tends to drive banks toward shortening that time horizon. In the end, we ended up incurring massive costs for the safety net because, as it turned out, the tail was much fatter and longer than people had thought.

Moreover, globalization of financial activities meant that there were a lot of crisis spillovers, and that when countries try to activate fiscal backstops, one finds that a lot of the fiscal support leaks overseas. The typical case was Iceland, a country that actually had to pay a lot to support or help creditors of Icelandic banks in other countries. People ended up saying, 'never again.' So, regulators decided to strengthen capital requirements to minimize the cost to the safety net.

But the big question is by how much should capital requirements be raised? If you raise regulatory capital, but if the level was still below whatever economic capital the banks would have had anyway, in fact there is really no change in the safety of the system because it still does not cover the tail risks for systemic circumstances.

So what do you do? You may try to increase regulatory capital above economic capital, that is, to tell the banks to prepare themselves for these tail events so that capital would be there to absorb the losses even in extreme events. In that case, there is really no reason for these private institutions to be in the business, because if the risk-return profile of banks' activities remains the same and banks are asked to double the capital, what happens is that the return on capital halves. Given that the capital costs are externally determined, banks that cannot generate enough return on capital simply cannot stay in business over the long run. So what happens? Business models and conditions have to adjust until economic capital is greater than regulatory capital.

How can banks manage to do that? There are a couple of possibilities and the first is that banks try to increase the profits and increase the returns on their activity, i.e., increase the lending margin. Basically, what this requires would be that the amount of intermediation services that are provided in the economy be reduced, so that with less supply banks get higher prices—that is, fatter lending margins.

You can also try to increase the rent through restricting competition, which would pretty much amount to the same thing. Of course, reduced supply of intermediation service by banks will result in disintermediation and competition from non-regulated intermediaries. This would soften the impact of the restricted supply of bank intermediation. However, the downside of this adjustment is that the source of instability would shift to the shadow banking sectors. At the same time, in this process, borrowers like the SMEs that do not have direct access to the capital market and have to rely on bank intermediation would be hit most. This is a part of today's concerns.

Secondly, the banks may try to shift to a higher return business, which would invariably involve higher risk. This course of action would appear especially attractive for banks if the regulatory capital charges on such activities are low compared to what the banks themselves perceive them to be. But this results in an even fatter and longer tail risk. In fact, it is possible that the possibility of systemic crisis and the losses in these tail events would actually become bigger.

You do not want that, so what you then might do is to restrict what you think as being these high risk, high return activities and to limit the size of tail risk—for example, the Volker rule. In fact, what you are trying to do is to force the financial system into the first solution where you reduce the amount of intermediation and increase the margins.

This seems all well from a stability viewpoint. But there is a trade-off, so you have to make some decisions on that trade-off. However, there is one catch here: that we are in a globalized world with lots of cross-border activities. If we want to set global standards, remember that the economic conditions, risk return profile and institutions' business models are different from one country to another. This means that if you set one common standard globally, the regulatory capital that is ex ante lower than economic capital in one country may be ex ante higher in another. You do not want that either, so you try to fine-tune the whole system to make sure that it is well calibrated and there are no negative effects for all countries. But that is going to be extremely difficult, and probably will not work.

So, where do we go? Confronted with these choices, the standard advice that everybody—sorry to take this potshot—including the IMF tells you is that you must come out with a well-balanced regulation that manages all these trade-offs nicely. The problem is, can you actually come up with a good solution that would manage the trade-off? Now many of you will have seen this impossible trinity diagram (Fig. 3, top left corner) that can be found in international finance textbooks or macro textbooks, showing that a country cannot have capital mobility, a fixed exchange rate, and independent monetary policy at the same time.

I posit that there is a similar impossible trinity among the three things that we all cherish in financial regulation and supervision. The first is globalization, that is to have liberalized, cross-border activity that is regulated by common rules. That would allow efficient allocation of resources internationally and would help emerging countries' growth.

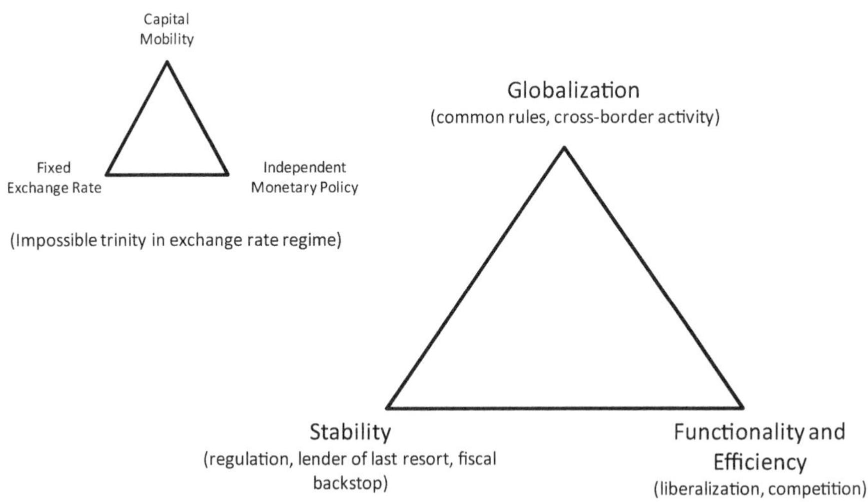

Fig. 3 Have your cake and eat it too? Impossible trinity of financial regulation. (Source: Author)

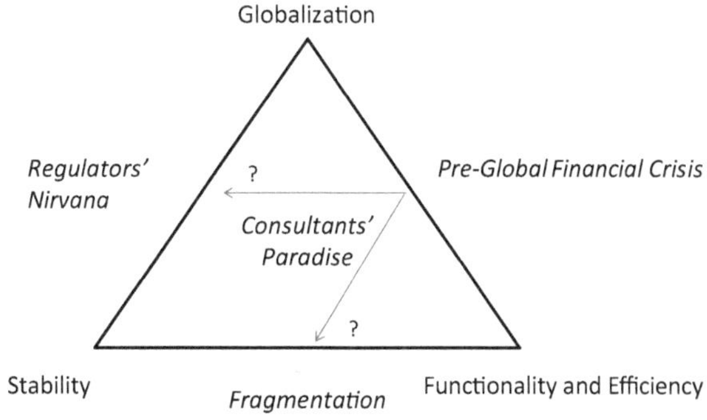

Fig. 4 Striking an appropriate balance. No happy middle ground? (Source: Author)

The second, on the bottom right-hand side, is what I term functionality and efficiency. As Ratna pointed out, liberalization and competition would bring greater and better provision of financial services. The third, on the bottom left, is stability. This may be achieved through strengthened regulation, but it is also possible to ensure ultimate stability through provision of fiscal backstops and lender of last resort functions.

An important observation that I would like to make concerning stability is that if we have a common, global fiscal backstop and a global lender of last resort, we may be able to achieve this stability, but if we could only have national fiscal backstops and lender of last resort, then stability would be extremely difficult to achieve in a globalized financial market.

Now let me illustrate in reference to this financial impossible trinity where we are and where we may go (Fig. 4). The pre-GFC state can be characterized, I think, by globalization combined with liberalization or light touch regulation. This system is not able to really deliver stability, or rather, whatever stability we did ultimately secure was gained through large fiscal cost at the national level. However, we have decided we are no longer willing to pay those huge costs.

So how can we choose stability, if a global fiscal backstop and lender of last resort is not possible? We could strengthen regulation while maintaining common global rules, and we may thus be able to regulate instability out of existence. But that is going to come at the cost of giving up efficiency and functionality of free markets. I have termed this solution "the regulators' nirvana" as regulators will end up enjoying perfect stability, but they have largely eliminated the financial system that they are supposed to regulate.

The second solution is for countries to put emphasis on optimizing their own trade-offs, and create their own rules if the international rules that they prefer cannot be agreed on. This would increasingly fragment the different national markets, and I think we are seeing a trend in this direction as different rules are being proposed and introduced in different jurisdictions.

Now, in practice, the world would not, and cannot, go to a total separation of national markets, so will end up with something in the middle, which I have termed the "Consultants' Paradise." As rules become more complicated and potentially conflicting, and since some regulator may resort to extra-territorial application of domestic regulation in order to secure effectiveness, a lot of interpretation will be needed on how national rules are going to be implemented and applied to cross-border institutions and activities. This is not a particularly pleasing situation for anyone, save financial industry consultants. The increased regulatory complexity will create room for regulatory arbitrage and might increase the risk, or create new risk, for financial stability.

So what is the solution? I am sorry that I have no good solution to address these problems. An academic can always shout out the problems loudly but just mumble the solutions. Professor Yoshino has long advocated different capital levels for different countries. I am sympathetic to the idea, but at the same time it is going to be difficult to apply them consistently to, for example, cross-border activity. Just think of trade financing between two firms in two countries financed by multiple banks in different countries and what that may involve in terms of applying regulation. Moreover, if you want to enforce such differentiated capital rules, you would probably need tighter regulation on who can do what in terms of cross-border activity, and that means capital controls may need to be a part of the regulatory set up.

While academics can simply raise questions, I know practitioners are not so lucky and I have great sympathy for those officials who have to navigate these trade-offs. Worse, it would be lucky if it were only an impossible trinity so that you need to sacrifice one of the three goals, but it might even be the case that the situation is actually a trilemma and that only one goal is achievable.

So with that depressing note, I would like to stop. Thank you very much.

Comments to Session 1

Tokio Morita

Thank you. It is a great pleasure and honor to be invited to the conference and to be given an opportunity to make comments after the two distinguished speakers.

Competition and Stability Are Two Important Policy Objectives

Ensuring financial system stability and fostering competition in the financial industry are the two important policy objectives of the regulatory authorities. For example, the mission statement of the Financial Services Agency, Japan, is:

1. Ensuring stability of the financial system;
2. Protection of users and improvement of convenience;
3. Establishing a fair and transparent market.

While "competition" is not explicitly mentioned, its importance is implied for the improvement of convenience and for achieving an efficient market.

However, this mission statement does not tell us anything about whether they are mutually consistent or contradictory, or what emphasis should be placed on each of the three. That may be today's topic.

Financial Deregulation and Financial System Crisis

The balance between competition and stability may change, depending on the circumstances. However, there is one thing that does not change. The regulators are always criticized for protecting banks too much. In a boom, banks make high profits. People criticize regulators for allowing banks to earn too much, increasing the economic rent through lack of sufficient competition due to restrictive regulations. On such occasions, banks also want to expand their scope for business operations to earn more. Thus, there is a strong driving force for deregulation to enhance competition. When the economy turns bad and we have a financial crisis, the regulators are criticized for protecting banks too much or for bailing them out.

Ms. Sahay pointed out that the empirical and theoretical literature has been ambiguous on whether competition is good or bad for financial stability. As a supervisor, I am not sure about the causality, but there seems to be a historical pattern of financial deregulation before a financial crisis, and macroeconomic factors also play a role. Before the current crisis, there was the Gramm-Leach-Bliley Act, which relaxed restrictions on banks' activities. In 1990s, there was the Japanese Financial System Crisis, and the Japanese government had initiated a package of financial deregulations that started in the mid-1980s. In 1980s, there was a Savings and Loans Crisis in the US after the interest rate deregulation. So, the question would be: can we have both competition and stability? Are regulators repeating the same mistakes again and again?

Regulations Are Evolving

One excuse for regulators will be that the regulations are evolving away from the direct restrictions on entry, activities, and interest rates toward ensuring sound risk management of banks through appropriately incentivizing banks. Deregulation of direct restrictions to foster competition should not mean no regulation, but that regulation is transformed into a different shape. The regulators are more mindful now of (i) transparency, (ii) cost-benefit analysis of the regulations, (iii) proportionality, (iv) competition neutrality, and (v) accountability. The policy objective of bank regulation has shifted away from preventing bank failure to effective crisis management.

The regulators take it for granted that bank failure, through greater competition and mismanagement, will not be totally avoided, and on that basis the regulators have been trying to contain the adverse impact of bank failure so that it will not cause a systemic crisis. As Ms. Sahay indicated, ending too-big-to-fail is important in this context. The Japanese FSA's "Better Regulation Initiative" is in line with this trend.

Banks are expected to establish sustainable business models to compete while having a robust risk management system in place. The proper and consistent implementation of international standards is important. The current Basel framework permits banks to use their own internal models to calculate risk-weighted assets, but the opaqueness and lack of comparability of the calculation is criticized. The incentives for banks should be the right ones. Basel Committee analysis confirmed the divergence of the calculation among banks on the same hypothetical portfolio. How to make the regulation simpler and more comparable is now on the agenda of the Basel Committee.

Supervision Is Also Changing

Even if that problem is rectified, as Mr. Ariyoshi pointed out, capital regulation may not be a panacea. If we tried to ensure financial system stability only with capital regulation, the regulation may be excessive, harm the competition, and kill the economy. This may be particularly so for Asian countries, which have a bank-centric financial system. Ms. Sahay suggested the importance of intensive supervision, and I fully agree with her. Supervision is changing after the Lehman crisis, away from the light touch supervision to intensive supervision, with more focus on the macroeconomy.

1. Basel III framework provides supervisors with a *countercyclical capital buffer framework.*
2. The *role of macroprudential supervision* is now much stressed. I understand the Hong Kong Monetary Authority, Monetary Authority of Singapore, and other Asian jurisdictions have taken such measures in light of recent real estate market developments.
3. *Stress testing* is more widely used. Some authorities use a supervisory stress test to ensure that banks have robust, forward-looking capital planning processes that account for the unique risks and need for sufficient capital to continue operations through times of economic and financial stress.
4. *Global cooperation* among supervisors is evolving *through supervisory colleges.* A supervisory college is established for each G-SIFI where supervisors exchange information, views, and concerns, and discuss whether any coordinated efforts are necessary.
5. *A robust framework to end too-big-to-fail is now being prepared.* An operational resolution plan that enables the resolution authorities to wind down a failed bank in an orderly manner will be ready for each G-SIB. The resolvability assessment will be conducted in cooperation with the IMF.

What Is Most Important Is the Self-Discipline of Bank Managers

In addition to these supervisory efforts, self-discipline of bank managers is important. Banks should have a solid corporate governance, proper risk appetite and culture, and remuneration policy. Banks should establish sustainable business models under the new regulatory regime. The banks' senior management should strongly commit to these objectives and the supervisors should discuss these issues with banks' top management regularly.

Deposit Guarantee Scheme and Resolution Fund as a Backstop

The effectiveness of these supervisory approaches has not been tested yet. Under this regime, we can still not eliminate failure of banks, and may not be able to avoid a future financial system crisis. Thus, it is our brief that, as a backstop, an adequate deposit guarantee scheme and a resolution fund are needed to cover the tail risk.

Shadow Banking Sector

Finally, let me briefly talk about the shadow banking sector. Japan has a bank-centric financial system and thus the last Japanese banking crisis had a huge impact on the real economy. I fully agree with Ms. Sahay on the idea that diversification of the financial system is important, and there should be a healthy competition between banks and non-banks. Non-banks should also be closely monitored, as it is not appropriate that the risk is just migrated from the heavily controlled banking sector to the non-regulated shadow banking sector. At the same time, it should be noted that the shadow banking sector is still in the development stage in many of the Asian countries, and the picture of the sector is rather different from the one in the US and Europe. It is important that the Asian views are also heard in the discussions of the standard setting bodies.

Conclusion

Let me conclude:

1. To strike a balance between competition and stability is a challenge. The nature of the regulations is changing, and the role of supervision and the self-discipline of bank management are coming to the fore.
2. However, the effectiveness of the new approach has not been well tested yet. Another full-scale financial crisis may not be avoidable. An adequate deposit guarantee scheme and a resolution fund are needed as a backstop.

3. Healthy competition between banks and non-banks may contribute to overall financial stability. The difference in the size and nature of the shadow banking sector between Asia and US/Europe should not be overlooked, and we should pay attention to these differences in the context of the standard setting bodies' discussions.

Akihiko Kagawa

Good afternoon. Thank you for giving me this opportunity to speak with you today. As a member of one of Japan's major financial institutions, I would like to comment on our future strategies in the current regulatory environment.

Current Regulatory Environment

First, I believe that the current regulatory environment has been strongly influenced by authorities in developed countries as countermeasures to problems that surfaced during the Global Financial Crisis in 2008.

These include:

1. Regulations governing complex derivatives and securitization products which were directly responsible for some of the enormous losses;
2. A requirement to maintain enough liquidity to protect against asset price volatility;
3. Capital enhancement as a loss-absorbing buffer;
4. Strengthening of controls against so-called conduct risks; and
5. Establishment of effective governance.

All of these are very important, and I have no objection to the current regulatory direction. However, there are underlying issues faced by financial institutions that need to be taken into account. I would like to spend a few minutes describing these issues.

First, the regulations impose enormous costs on financial institutions. This includes the cost of establishing the structures to properly respond to the regulations, the costs to individual business that arise from qualitative changes in the market, and capital costs. How to cover these expenses is a vexing question, as under normal circumstances they would cause a decline of profitability.

Second, financial institutions will tend to adopt slow and stagnant strategies because of the restrictive nature of these regulations. All of these regulatory measures can trigger the contraction of risk amount and asset volume. All of these factors, together with the costs, make it difficult for us to sustain and increase our corporate value.

The third issue is the basic lack of fairness in the competitive environment caused by non-banks or shadow banks. Further, it is reasonable to assume that the potential exists for new financial risks that could arise from these entities. Given the ongoing super monetary easing policies in developed countries, I believe that an enormous amount of money is building up or circulating in this sector. We need adequate safeguards to prevent another financial crisis and to protect our customers.

Strategies for Financial Institutions

Next, I would like to talk about what kind of strategies, under these circumstances, will need to be developed by financial institutions like Mitsubishi UFJ Financial Group (MUFG).

The first is establishing a customer-first corporate culture that enjoys the trust and confidence of both society and our customers. We must develop business strategies that are consistent with this kind of culture and we must make meaningful contributions to the real business both in domestic and overseas businesses.

Second, we must expand our business in a sustainable manner and have a philosophy based on long-term relationships that does not focus on short-term profits. This is crucial if we want to maintain and improve the trust and confidence our customers have in us.

Third, we should have a business that uses a risk appetite framework effectively to create an environment that is well balanced between offense and defense. We will still need to make judgments on downsizing or other negative actions if we encounter problems that can potentially affect our sustainability. However, it is more important that we manage working capital by following a sound and effective risk appetite framework. This is because if we want to maintain financial soundness amid growing costs, we cannot accept any unexpected losses.

Our Views on Our Competition

Finally, I would like to touch upon our views on the competitive environment.

So far, it may have sounded to you like Mitsubishi UFJ Financial Group is a bit negative toward the competition in the financial market. However, we are not. Based upon our value and philosophy, as I already mentioned, we are determined to enhance our corporate value by surviving healthy competition with other financial institutions. I believe it is entirely possible for us to acquire more business opportunities if we firmly establish a corporate culture that focuses on a customer-first philosophy and values the trust and confidence of society and our customers. We are hopeful that our competitors will join us in contributing to a fair and sound market, which benefits the entire economic environment.

This concludes my presentation. Thank you.

Jae-Ha Park

First of all, I would like to thank FSA, Japan and the IMF for organizing this event together with ADBI. Following last year's important achievements, I think it is a very good new occasion for us to discuss financial system stability and competition in many areas.

I think the two speakers covered the important aspects of financial stability and competition after the Global Financial Crisis well. Of course they could not cover all areas and all aspects of the financial reform processes after the Global Financial Crisis. Instead, they selected some important topics concerning financial stability and concentrated on competition issues. I am briefly summarizing the papers of Dr. Sahay and Dr. Ariyoshi.

First of all, Dr. Sahay's main message includes, first, that competition improves financial access and reduces financing costs. However, to reap the benefits from competition, regulation and supervision need to be strengthened to capture potential new risks. Second, regulatory standards have to be applied consistently between banks and non-banks. Third, coordination and consultation mechanisms would need to exist between the prudential and competitive authorities. Of course, her presentation included many other important lessons and policy prescriptions.

Dr. Ariyoshi covered many issues using the concepts of economic capital and regulatory capital. Detailed regulations and a high degree of calibration are necessary to ensure that common global standards can provide a level playing field.

He also mentioned the impossible trinity problem among globalization, stability, and functionality and efficiency. Regarding those important messages by two eminent speakers, I have noted their views and objections, but I would like to add a couple of other important issues based on their presentations.

First of all, we all know that within the financial regulatory reform process after the Global Financial Crisis, diverse financial reform measures have been taken by various organizations and countries to make financial systems more resilient and better able to serve the needs of the real economy. Under the umbrella of the G20, many organizations like the Financial Stability Board (FSB), the BIS, the standard setting bodies, and also the IMF, the World Bank, and other multilateral development banks, as well as global forums like the Financial Action Task Force and FSB, have contributed to making the global financial system more stable and more resilient.

On the issues, the key areas of the regulatory reform include, first, Basel III capital adequacy norms; second, the systemic risk issue on SIFIs; third, the shadow banking issues, which were also covered by my colleague from the FSA in Japan; and fourth, the Glass–Steagall Act, the Volcker Rule, and the Vickers and Liikanen proposals—the acts have been discussed although they are not yet enacted. Also the over-the-counter derivatives markets have been widely discussed and recent compensation practices in many other important areas and in many countries have been discussed.

Consumer protection has, among others, become a very important issue for financial reform processes and also to strengthen supervision, so it was widely discussed how to strengthen national regulatory oversight. Also on the regulation issues, living wills and bail-in issues have been discussed, as well as the financial sector assessment programs through the IMF and the Financial Stability Board.

The G20 has already reached several important agreements to enhance global financial regulatory reforms, but much remains to be finalized and the speed of the financial reform is quite slow. So I would like to pick up on a few of the issues from the two speakers' presentations.

First of all, on the benefits and costs of new financial regulations. It is widely expected that financial reform efforts will bring about substantial benefits by reducing the risk of financial crises, by enhancing the resilience of banks and other financial institutions in case crises do arise, and by reducing economic volatility and increasing transparency.

However, it may come at the price of increased costs for financial intermediation. As an example of some research, Elliott, Salloy, and Santos (Elliott et al. 2012) estimate that current financial reforms may raise the lending rates 18 basis points (bps) in Europe, 8 bps in Japan, and 28 bps in the US in the long run. So the question of whether the benefits of financial reform outweigh its costs depends on how well new financial regulations work in reducing risks.

The second issue is the relationship between competition and stability. It is true that empirical and theoretical literature has provided ambiguous findings and predictions on the relationship between competition and financial stability, as was well explained by Dr. Sahay. However, the many experiences of financial crises in the advanced countries and developing countries, in particular in the East Asian countries during the late 1990s, show that rapid and excessive financial liberalization and market opening without proper financial regulation and supervision weakened the soundness and stability of the financial system, and eventually created financial crises.

The key question is whether strong and intensive financial regulation and supervision are working efficiently in the economy, rather than the level of competition policies themselves.

The third issue is the relationship between the prudential and the competition authorities. In many cases, the objectives and interests of competition authorities are quite different and even in many cases conflicting with those of the prudential authorities. For example, competition authorities put greater emphasis on more competition, thereby increasing the efficiency and competitiveness of the financial industries. However, the prudential authorities put more emphasis on stability and soundness of the financial system. A strong coordination and consultation mechanism has to be present and is quite necessary, and I totally agree with Dr. Sahay on this point. However, we must note that particularly during normal times, during peacetime with no signs of crises, the voices of the competition authorities are usually much stronger than those of the prudential authorities.

We must be very careful, therefore, about these kinds of strong coordination and cooperation. So in some ways, I think personally, some kind of tension and conflicting views between these two authorities may be necessary, ironically.

The fourth issue is the need for international coordination. International coordination in financial regulation is indispensable to limit the scope for arbitrage opportunities among internationally operating SIFIs in particular. Thus, international cooperation at the regional level is also important to reduce the risk of cross-border distortion and spillover arising from unilateral actions by neighboring countries.

My final point concerns the application of common global standards to emerging market economies. The application of common global standards may cause some problems for emerging market economies that have considerably different financial systems from those in advanced economies. For example, the higher capital requirement rules could prompt banks of emerging economies to raise capital ratios much above the minimum level, which could have negative impacts on loan growth. New liquidity standards may also constrain bank lending in the emerging economies, where bank lending is the main source of credit.

And finally, new rules for global SIFIs may constrain lending growth in host economies. So international organizations should take into account emerging economies' special considerations and concerns in designing new international financial standards and policies.

Thank you.

Open Floor Discussion

Naoyuki Yoshino: Thank you very much for the very stimulating discussions. I would like to ask especially Deputy Director Ratna Sahay about the background of these crises. We often observe much liquidity in certain countries, before turnover on the stock market increases and land and house prices start to rise. If those data can be observed as an early warning system, would it be possible to strengthen the supervision and regulations for financial structure based on those data? Then you can change the regulations and supervision based on those macroeconomic figures. Would it be possible to do so to avoid a crisis? Thank you.

Ratna Sahay: Thank you very much for asking that question. One of the realizations that came after this crisis was indeed that if you want to meet the goals of macroeconomic stability and financial stability, it is not enough just to have monetary policy and fiscal policy, because those two meet macro-stability goals. To get financial stability, you need macro prudential policies. On the specific issue that you are pointing to, a lot of studies have been done. There is in fact very robust empirical evidence showing that a very rapid increase in credit and housing prices is a very good predictor of crisis.

So I definitely think the IMF, but also other national authorities, are now setting up, if they do not already have them, national financial stability boards for monitoring these developments in the financial sector; and they are also empowering their prudential, macro-prudential authorities to give advice and take action preemptively.

The second thing that we have found is that the macro-prudential policies, like the ratios that are imposed on loans as a share of income of households, for example, are much more effective if they are introduced before a crisis, so pre-emptively, in a precautionary way. A lot of countries are doing that. In fact, many countries in Asia are doing that and it has proved very useful.

But one last point I do want to make is that even if you have macro-prudential policies, if capital flows are very large and very sudden, they can also completely overwhelm the macro-prudential policies.

Odd Per Brekk: Thank you very much, Ratna. I have been struck listening to you on this question of international collaboration and especially the comments by Professor Ariyoshi. To what extent are cross-border considerations really effectively included in the policy agenda for regulatory reforms? Are spillovers taken into account or is the need for consistency taken into account?

You very often hear, I think, when you go to meetings and so on in Asia, authorities complain that their voice is not being heard. Similarly, when you look at or read about the Vickers, Volcker, and Liikanen structural measures, it looks like very different approaches are adopted in different countries. So is this taken into account? To what extent is it taken into account or is it even possible, as Akira was perhaps hinting it might not be? I guess it may be a question for Ratna, and maybe also for Mr. Morita.

Ratna Sahay: You are not supposed to ask me difficult questions since we are from the same organization. I think, Odd, it poses a very important question and indeed it is a difficult question. To be very frank with you, this is an area where we have not made much progress on the cross-border issues. It is not for lack of trying. These are really on top of the agenda of the FSB and other international bodies. But I think this is one area where a lot more progress needs to be made. Because it is very hard to reconcile very different structural models of different countries. This is why already there are differences in advanced economies.

Then if you add the emerging markets and the low-income countries, the landscape becomes even more different. If we are not able to do it, as we heard from Professor Ariyoshi, we will have financial fragmentation. That is how it is going to end up. So to benefit from globalization, I think we have to keep going at it very consistently. As you know, some progress has been made. For example, the US and UK have come to an understanding on cross-border issues and one should be able to extend that more and more to other regions. But it is very much on the agenda and people are still working on it.

Akira Ariyoshi: I think it was more than 10 years ago that a law professor asked me about the legal set up for international financial regulation—Basel committee, and all that. He asked what legal legitimacy they have. He compared them with trade negotiations, saying that trade negotiations in any trade agreement have to be basically ratified by the parliament, as part of a political process. But then financial regulations—and even perhaps more so macroeconomic coordination—seem to be run by these G-somethings without any legal underpinnings. So, the question was, why is it that financial regulations can be decided on or agreed on at the international level through such a soft process?

The seat of my pants answer was that this is because the financial regulators all have a common view as to what is right. So we do the right thing and keep it away from the politicians who might have different ideas. The financial crisis has shown that financial regulators are not really doing the right thing. Their regulation was unable to prevent crisis. So the politicians have decided that financial regulation is too important to let regulators run it on their own. The whole process has become rightly or wrongly politicized. I think, increasingly, the issue will be about whether there is a conflict between national interest and global rules. And it is unfortunate, as I look at the international discussions on financial regulation, that it is beginning to look increasingly like trade negotiations.

The way the trade negotiations are going might present a picture of the future for financial regulation, and so does Ratna's comment about the US and UK—that is a free trade agreement, right? So rather than fragmentation along country lines we may have fragmentation at a regional level, with a group of countries adopting common regulations. Going back to the analogy of trade negotiations, the concern is whether we are going to have spaghetti bowls or, in the case of Asia, noodle bowls of financial regulation.

Tokio Morita: The importance of the consistent implementation of the global standard is pretty much recognized in the international forums. In particular, a Basel committee has started the regulatory consistency assessment program, which has three layers. Level I is the timing, Level II is the regulatory consistency, and Level III is at the banks' level because banks are, as I said, permitted to use their own internal models. That is one thing. The FSB will also start the resolvability assessment to check whether each restriction meets the key attributes of the resolution regime.

You mentioned the structural reform in banks. This is my personal opinion, but this originated from three questions. One is whether the regulatory authorities can have full confidence in proper risk management of banks. The second is the capacity of the supervisory authorities, whether we can effectively combat and monitor the supervision over the banks' risk management. Third is the resolvability. If the banks get complex, however, it is very hard to resolve them.

But if we try to ensure consistency from the viewpoint of the regulating field, that may be a little tricky, because when we talk about the resolution, the resolution or deposit guarantee schemes are different from jurisdiction to jurisdiction. We cannot have a unique international resolution scheme, so to some extent some kind of flexibility should be maintained. Thank you.

Anthony Rowley: Anthony Rowley, Singapore Business Times, a very simplistic question. How meaningful are capital-to-risk-asset ratios when risk seems to be so complex and difficult to measure? Each time there is a financial crisis, it turns out that, because of the complexity of the system, capital is hopelessly inadequate. So is there some other ratio that should be adopted that could reflect risk more realistically?

Odd Per Brekk: Anyone who wants to take that question?

Ratna Sahay: Let me just make one comment and then the others can. In my view, one key issue that we have not resolved—and I think that should be addressed and I understand there is a lot of thought going into it—is banks differ quite a lot in their internal risk models. I think we need to have some ways to give the right incentives to these banks to ensure that the risk models actually truly reflect the risks. There is nothing wrong with banks having their own models. But then it should reflect the risks of these models. So that is one aspect.

The second aspect, of course, is getting the accounting standards, which should also be addressed. Because measuring, as you rightly point out, is the first step to recognizing the risk, and we have not fully addressed this. But we are on the way, I think.

Akira Ariyoshi: I would say that finding a good regulatory ratio is the Holy Grail of financial regulation. If you look at history, remember we started off with a simple leveraged regulation back in the 1970s. Then the argument was that it does not really account for risk, so we put in Basel I. Then that was seen to be too crude, as there were a lot of arbitrage opportunities. Then we put in the Basel IIs and IIIs. Then after that, we realized we need to ask whether risk measurements by individual institutions are really right or consistent. Now people are trying to bring back the simple leverage ratios.

My sense of this is that risk management at the individual institutional level, as I said in my comments, is not really risk management but essentially earnings management: that banks try to reduce the volatility of earnings while maximizing returns. Fundamentally, I think banks' internal risk management it is not really suited for capturing tail risks and major systemic risks. So there is a fundamental disconnect there and that is my point.

But then at the same time I am not quite sure that there is a particularly good method or good ratios that would help regulators maintain a stable financial system. Because the truth is that the usefulness of any ratio disappears as soon as you put it into a regulatory framework. So I think that would be my very pessimistic conclusion, which I can state only because I am no longer a regulator.

Tokio Morita: We know that the capital ratio has been criticized on many points. My point is that some holistic approach may be necessary and we cannot just rely on capital ratios. For example, Basel III introduced a liquidity ratio as well as a capital ratio. As Mr. Ariyoshi pointed out, our capital ratio is a lagged indicator and as such it may not have helped to predict the crisis. In response, some authorities, as I said, have started using their strength testing as a supervisory tool. Intensive supervision is also important, but above all it is not the regulators who run the banks but the bank managers, so self-discipline is very important.

I sincerely hope that our new regulatory approach will work, but we will see. Thank you.

Odd Per Brekk: Thank you very much. I think we will stop here unless any of the panelists or discussants want to add anything. Let me thank you very much. I will resist the temptation to try and summarize this very broad-ranging discussion. In any event, there will be a policy panel at the end of the day chaired by Dean Kawai, which will try in effect to draw together some of the strands of this discussion and the ones that will follow later today.

References

Claessens S, Laeven L (2005) Financial dependence, banking sector competition, and economic growth. Policy Research Working Paper Series 3481. World Bank, Washington, DC

Claessens S (2009) Competition in the financial sector: overview of competition policies. IMF Working Paper 09/45. International Monetary Fund, Washington, DC

Elliott D, Salloy S, Santos A (2012) Assessing the cost of financial regulation. IMF Working Paper No. WP/12/233. International Monetary Fund, Washington, DC

FSB (2013) Update on financial regulatory factors affecting the supply of long-term investment finance. Report to G20 Finance Ministers and Central Bank Governors

IMF (2012a) Changing global financial structures: can they improve economic outcomes? (Chap. 4). Global Financial Stability Report, October 2012. International Monetary Fund, Washington, DC

IMF (2012b) The reform agenda: an interim progress report toward a safer financial system (Chap. 3). Global Financial Stability Report, October 2012. International Monetary Fund, Washington, DC

IMF (2013a) Global financial stability report. International Monetary Fund, Washington, DC

IMF (2013b) Key aspects of macroprudential policies. IMF Policy Paper. International Monetary Fund, Washington, DC

IMF, BIS, FSB (2009) Guidance to assess the systemic importance of financial institutions, markets and instruments: initial considerations. Report to the G20 Finance Ministers and Governors

Noss J, Sowerbutts R (2012) The implicit subsidy of banks. Bank of England Financial Stability Paper No. 15

OECD (2011) Bank competition and financial stability. OECD, Paris

Ratnovski L (2013) Competition policy for modern banks. IMF Working Paper 13/126. International Monetary Fund, Washington, DC

Viñals J, Fiechter J (2010) The making of good supervision: learning to say "no." IMF staff position note 10/08. International Monetary Fund, Washington, DC

Viñals J, Pazarbasioglu C, Surti J, Narain A, Erbenova M, Chow J (2013) Creating a safer financial system: will the Volcker, Vickers, and Liikanen structural measures help? IMF Staff Discussion Note 13/4. International Monetary Fund, Washington, DC

World Bank (2013) The role of the state in promoting bank competition (Chap. 3). Global Financial Development Report 2013. World Bank, Washington, DC

Keynote Speech: Current Situation, Challenges, and Future of Regional Finance in Japan

Hisashi Ono

Good afternoon, ladies and gentlemen. I hope you all feel refreshed from the lunch break. Before the break, we had a very interesting session focusing on financial system stability and competition in the financial services industry. In the afternoon, we will focus on the issue of financing for SMEs and financial inclusion.

To start the afternoon session, I would like to speak on regional finance in Japan. I will discuss three themes from the viewpoint of financial administration. First, the present situation of regional finance; then, the challenges based thereon; and finally, the future direction of regional financial institutions in meeting such challenges.

Present Situation of Japan's Regional Finance

First, I would like to explain the present situation of regional finance in Japan.

Please look at Fig. 1. It shows the year-on-year change in the amounts outstanding of loans to SMEs for the entire banking industry. The line shows the change in amounts outstanding of loans from the same period in the previous year. As you can see, amounts outstanding of loans had been declining year-on-year until recently. It finally turned positive in July 2013 and increased by 1.3 % in October 2013.

If we focus on regional banks, you can see that the amounts outstanding of loans to SMEs had been increasing year-on-year from a much earlier time. In other words, while the year-on-year change in amounts outstanding of loans to SMEs on a basis

The views expressed in this presentation are those of the author and do not necessarily reflect the views of the Financial Services Agency or the FSA Institute. See http://www.fsa.go.jp/frtc/english/katudou/conference/20140312.html.

H. Ono
Supervisory Bureau, Financial Services Agency, 3-2-1 Kasumigaseki, Chiyoda-ku, 100-8967 Tokyo, Japan

ADB Institute, Financial Services Agency, Japan, International Monetary Fund Regional Office for Asia and the Pacific (eds.), *Financial System Stability, Regulation, and Financial Inclusion,* ADB Institute Series on Development Economics, DOI 10.1007/978-4-431-55254-3_3

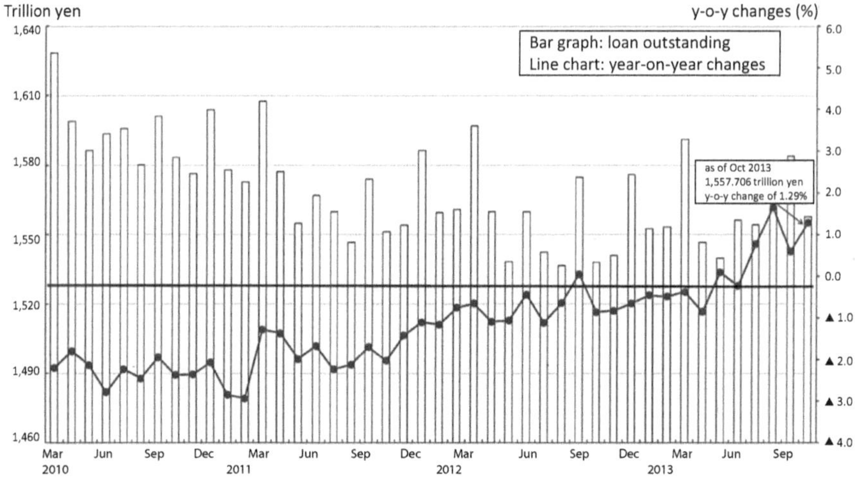

Fig. 1 Bank loans to small and medium-sized enterprises. (Source: Amount outstanding of loans is calculated from the total of loans to small and medium-sized enterprises by "city banks," "regional banks," and "regional banks II" in the Bank of Japan's statistics for "Deposits, Vault Cash, and Loans and Bills Discounted")

including megabanks is negative, such change on a basis excluding megabanks has been positive in recent years.

Regional banks have increased amounts outstanding of loans to SMEs in the regions damaged by the Great East Japan Earthquake.

Looking at developments in loans in the slightly longer term, we can observe certain tendencies in regional banks' loans, deposits, and loan-to-deposit ratios (Fig. 2). Amounts outstanding of loans have increased by approximately 34 trillion yen in the last 10 years, and deposits have increased even more, by approximately 58 trillion yen in the same period. As a result, the loan-to-deposit ratio has declined by approximately 2 %.

The same tendency can be seen in credit associations and credit unions, which are smaller regional banks. Their loans outstanding have increased, but this has been outstripped by an increase in deposits. As a result, the loan-to-deposit ratio has declined.

Next, let us take a look at the profits of regional banks, credit associations, and credit unions (Fig. 3). The capital adequacy ratios of regional banks have been stable at over 11 % on average, much higher than the required 4 % or more according to the Basel rules for domestic banks (on a Basel II requirement basis). The bad loan ratio has also declined and has been around 3 %. Banks look sound and well, but a question comes to our mind. Are financial institutions really making profits? To answer this question, we have to look at an important concept called "net operating profits from core business," which are banks' profits excluding gains or losses from

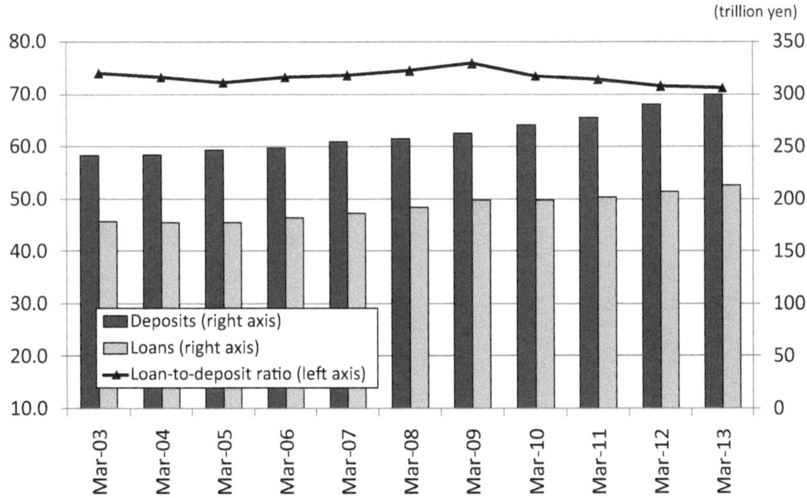

Deposits (right axis)	241.2	241.8	246.0	248.0	254.0	257.3	262.1	270.4	277.2	289.5	298.9
Loans (right axis)	178.3	177.2	177.7	181.7	186.6	191.4	198.6	198.4	201.5	206.6	212.5
Loan-to-deposit ratio (left axis)	73.9	73.3	72.2	73.3	73.5	74.4	75.8	73.4	72.7	71.4	71.1

Fig. 2 Deposits, loans, and loan–deposit ratios of regional banks. (Source: Figures are calculated based on the statistics of the Japanese Bankers Association)

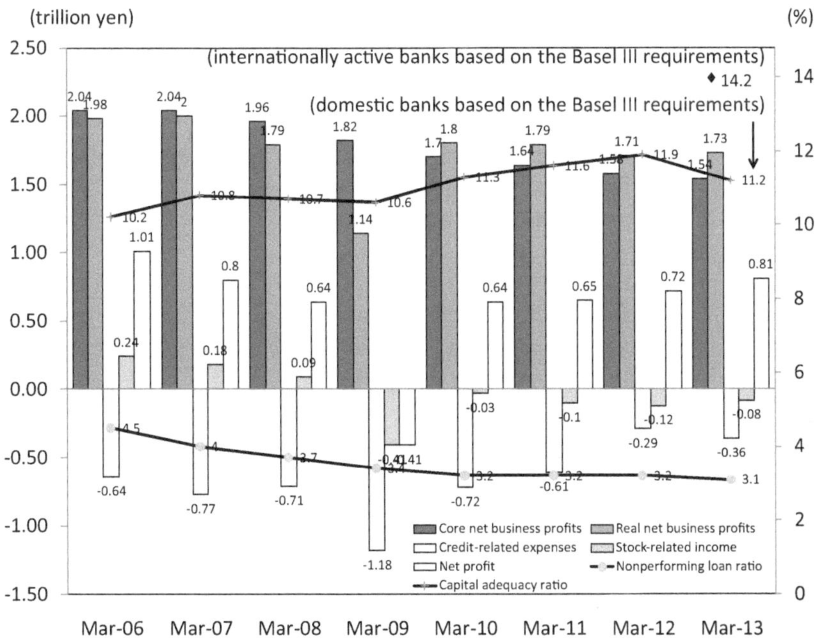

Fig. 3 Regional banks' financial statements. Notes: (1) Capital adequacy ratios from March 2006 to March 2009 do not include Ashikaga Bank, which was under special public management during that period. (2) Operating profits from core business are equal to operating profits excluding realized gains/losses on Japanese government bond holdings. (Source: Japanese Bankers Association)

bond and other trading. In other words, the concept shows banks' profits from their core business, such as lending.

Regional banks' net operating profits from core business have been declining, and similar tendencies can be seen for credit associations and credit unions (pp. 9–10). With regard to credit associations and credit unions, given that a substantial amount of their loans are to SMEs and smaller firms, their bad loan ratios are slightly higher than for other banks, but both bad loan ratios and capital adequacy ratios are stable. However, core net operating profits have been declining, like those for regional banks.

Now let us move on the second subject.

Challenges for Regional Finance

One of the important challenges for financial institutions now is the decline in loan-to-deposit ratios. Competition among regional financial institutions has grown fiercer. Regional financial institutions are now expanding beyond their own prefectures or areas and have begun operating in other regions. As a result, competition has become extremely fierce. This has resulted in a decline in lending rates and, subsequently, lower profit margins. In tandem with this, core net operating profits have also decreased. As financial institutions cannot increase lending, they are purchasing more Japanese government bonds for investment. This means that they are exposed to interest rate risk. If Japanese government bond (JGB) prices fall, financial institutions holding a large amount of JGBs could suffer significant unrealized or realized capital loss.

If we look at loan-to-deposit ratios by region, the ratio of some areas used to be over 100 %. That is, banks in such areas used to lend more money than they collected as deposits. However, the ratios have now dropped below 100 %, to around 70 %, even in the Tokyo metropolitan area and the Kansai area (the metropolitan area in the western part of Japan). In some other areas, the ratios are 50–60 %. This explicitly shows that loan-to-deposit ratios are declining.

If we look at the flow of funds table for Japan, we can see that savings account for more than half of all Japanese financial assets, and these savings flow into national and local government bonds.

Let us now look at the breakdown of deposits in more detail (Fig. 4). The elderly have more deposits than younger people, which is natural considering Japan's low birthrate and aging population. In Japan, deposits held by people aged 60 years or older account for 62 % of all deposits. This has two implications for Japan's finance. First, we need to make sure that the deposits of the elderly are utilized for growth. And second, demographic shifts from here on will see deposits moving to cities from other regions through what are called "inheritance deposits." This is because when elderly people with large deposits pass away, the children who receive the inheritance are now likely to reside in a large urban area, such as in the Tokyo metropolitan area or the Kansai area. There are estimates that regional deposits will

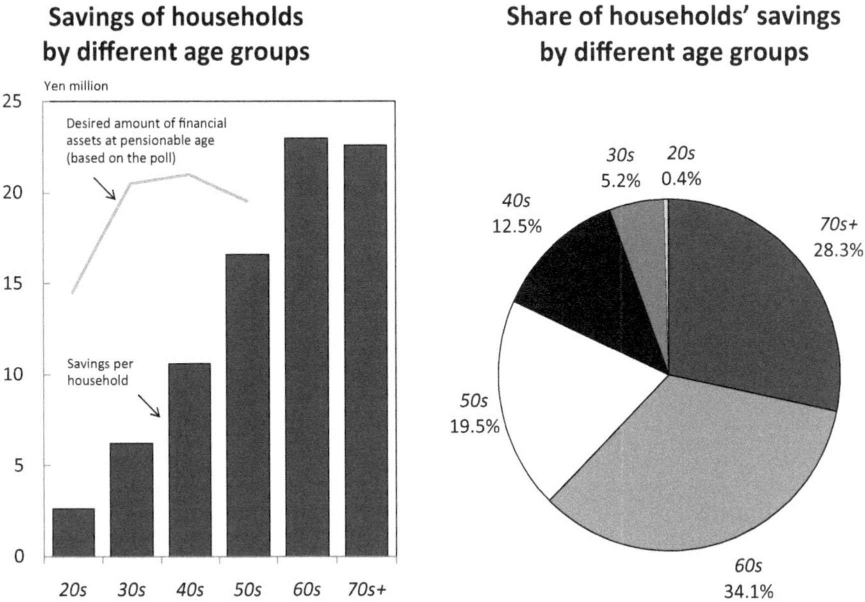

Fig. 4 Increasing importance of management of financial assets in aging Japan. (*Left*: Ministry of Internal Affairs and Communications. 2010. Family income and expenditure survey (savings and liabilities); Bank of Japan. 2010. Public opinion survey on household financial assets and liabilities. *Right*: Ministry of Internal Affairs and Communications. 2010. Family income and expenditure survey (savings and liabilities))

begin to decrease approximately 10 years after the population begins to decline in the region. Therefore, from now on, regional financial institutions will see deposits decreasing, especially in rural areas. It is a phenomenon they have never encountered before, and is one of the big challenges facing regional finance.

On the other hand, there are many vigorous companies in rural regions. More companies are advancing overseas in search of new business opportunities and are establishing overseas affiliated companies. Companies that are developing overseas business aggressively are mainly small firms with small capital. How to support such vigorous companies in Japan's rural regions is also a big challenge.

These challenges were closely studied in a report published in May 2012 by the Financial System Council's "Working Group on the Medium- and Long-Term Modalities of the Japanese Financial Industry," a body chaired by Professor Naoyuki Yoshino of Keio University. (It is available from the Financial Services Agency's website.) The report focused on three challenges: strengthening the international competitiveness of the Japanese financial industry, improving the financial intermediary function in regional economies, and providing financial services that meet the needs of the people. Issues that are particularly relevant to regional finance are the last two, namely the improvement in the financial intermediary function in regional economies and provision of financial services that meet the needs of the people.

Fig. 5 Toward a new financial industry. (Source: Author)

"The roles of the financial industry"

(1) To support the real economy
(2) To lead the economy as a growing industry itself

Toward a financial industry creating values that meet the needs of customers

Financial institutions are required to play roles such as:

- Fulfillment of the risk conversion function
- Function of the information transmission
- Execution of management strategies with a greater emphasis on the customer perspective
- Development and expansion of business foundations
- Nurturing of experts in finance

I will first discuss improvement in the financial intermediary function. The roles that the Japanese financial industry are required to play are risk conversion functions, information transmission functions, execution of management strategies with a greater emphasis on the customer perspective, development and expansion of business foundations including the financial condition, and the nurturing of experts in finance with the ability to discern the business potential of companies and industries (Fig. 5).

On the other hand, the challenges for regional economies are to rehabilitate and revive local SMEs, to revitalize rural communities, to promote new industries, and, as the population ages, to promote Compact City projects, or New Town Planning for elderly people. Amidst these challenges, the ways regional financial institutions can contribute are through their functions to convert risks, to utilize asset-based lending that does not depend on real estate for collateral, and to promote venture business through investment by funds instead of provisions of loans. It is also important that financial institutions improve information transmission functions, and support SMEs through collaborations between industry, academia, and the government. Financial institutions should also enhance human resources by nurturing specialists in specific fields who can discern the sustainable business potential of companies and industries and fully utilize outside experts.

I will now discuss the challenges involved in providing financial services that meet the needs of financial services users. The needs of customers are becoming more diversified nowadays, so, when developing financial products, financial institutions must gain a clear understanding of the needs of customer firms. Recently, there has been a concept called "value chain finance." This concept essentially hinges on whether financial institutions can enhance the value of customer enterprises based on a clear understanding of their values and needs. This is another reason why human resource development is crucial for financial institutions. In addition, the government also needs to remove factors that are preventing financial institutions from supplying funds for growth. Specifically, we are reviewing the "5 % rule" and other regulations on financial institutions' holdings of stocks with votes. We are also reviewing our inspection methods to enable financial institutions to perform an active financial intermediary function. In addition to these initiatives, Japan will introduce "NISA," the Japanese version of Individual Savings Accounts, in January 2014. In order to encourage individual savers to put more money into growth funds, NISA will offer tax-exemption on earnings of up to 1 million yen a year. The government is also looking into developing a more sophisticated risk management system in order to improve the investment performance of public funds.

Future of Regional Finance

Now I will move on to discuss the future of regional finance. There are two issues regarding what is expected for regional finance from now on. One is to strengthen support for improving the corporate structure and business management of regional firms that play vital roles in regional economies. And second is to provide credits and equity-like funds to growth industries that each regional economy has its strength in, such as agriculture and nursing care. For financial institutions, this means that they need to go back to the basics of their business, that is, to support and nurture firms. In line with this, we at the Financial Services Agency (FSA) are changing the way we conduct financial administration, and hence the method of financial inspection and supervision. Every fiscal year, the FSA prepares and publishes its basic policies for financial inspections and supervision. These inspection policies and supervisory policies outline how the FSA will perform financial inspections and financial supervision in that fiscal year. Fiscal year 2013 has seen a change in these policies. In the past, financial inspections had been performed from the viewpoint of whether financial institutions comply with laws and regulations and whether they meet the criteria stipulated in the Financial Inspection Manual. From this year onward, however, emphasis is placed more on how financial institutions are contributing to vitalizing regional economies and how they evaluate customer firms' financial conditions, not only their current financial data but also their business potential and technological capacities. The focus of FSA's inspections will be placed on the core issues of financial institutions' business management, and therefore for the evaluation of small-value assets. The FSA will respect financial institutions' internal evaluation of assets, instead of closely checking the adequacy of their evaluation.

As regards the supervisory policy, the policy for regional financial institutions for the current fiscal year states that supervision will focus on the primary roles of financial institutions, such as whether they are performing an active financial intermediary function like supporting the activities of SMEs and other businesses. To this end, the policy sets three areas to be emphasized in supervision, namely: promotion of initiatives for increasing new loans, deepening of region-based relationship banking, and support for the business improvement of SMEs (Fig. 6).

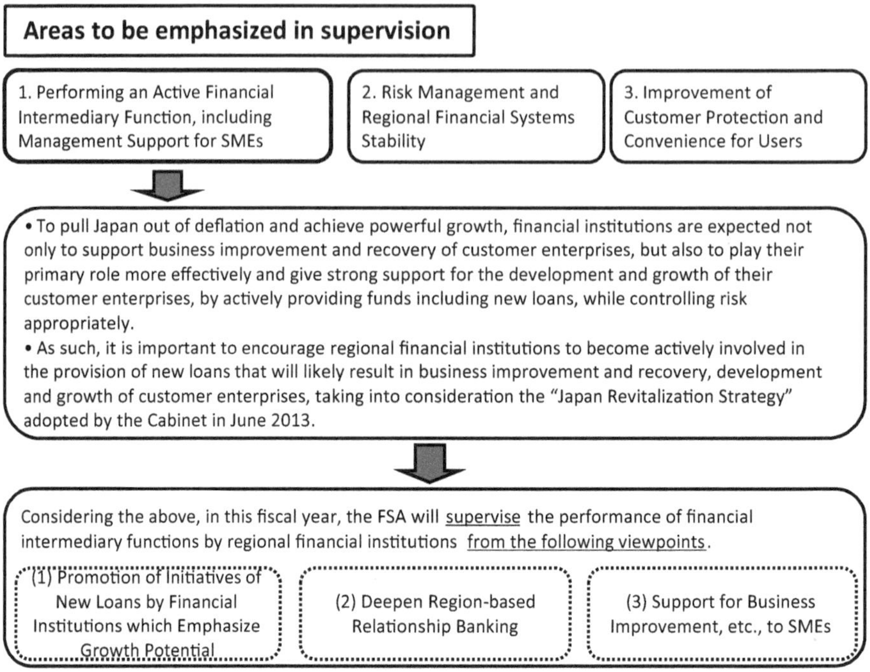

Fig. 6 Outline of the annual supervisory policy for regional financial institutions for fiscal year 2013. (Source: Financial Services Agency, Japan)

I will look at these three areas closely. The first is initiatives to increase loans. Through supervision, we check whether financial institutions regularly conduct analyses regarding business categories and regions with potential growth in money demand and set their strategy, policy, and goals for new loans based on the results of such analyses. We will also check whether financial institutions rely too easily on real estate for collateral or guarantees, and whether they take into account employees' efforts for increasing new loans in personnel evaluations.

As for the second area, region-based relationship banking, regional financial institutions have been taking measures for "relation banking" for over 10 years. However, financial institutions need to focus on not just financial matters of their customer firms, but should also look at firms' challenges in business matters by working with outside experts in order to propose optimum solutions to customers and help them implement these proposals. In other words, financial institutions need to pursue the Plan-Do-Check-Act (PDCA) cycle to help customer firms at different stages of their development. Financial institutions would have to grasp customer firms' situations and problems accurately, and then prepare and propose optimal solutions to the problems, and adopt these solutions with the customer and monitor their implementation, and where necessary, review and amend these solutions.

The third area is financial institutions' support for the business improvement of SMEs. Financial institutions will need to work harder to support SMEs' business

- On 18 March 2013, the Enterprise Turnaround Initiative Corporation of Japan was fundamentally reorganized and initiated operations with expanded functions as the **Regional Economy Vitalization Corporation of Japan (REVIC)**.

- The objective of **REVIC** is to vitalize regional economies through the formation of groups of healthy companies and the securing/creation of jobs by providing support for business turnaround based on selection and concentration of business and business restructuring; and support for starting up new business/implementing business change, and regional revitalization projects.

- Main Functions

  (1) Direct support for business turnaround
  - Deadline for deciding support:end of March 2018
  - Support period: "less than 5 years"
  - In the case of a large company, the name of the company will be publicly announced.

  (2) Enhancement of regional revitalization ability
  - Enhancement of cooperation such as dispatching experts to the SME Business Rehabilitation Support Cooperatives and to regional financial institutions
  - Dispatch of experts to, and capital injection/loans to, subsidiaries for business turnaround
  - Dispatch of experts and capital injection for business turnaround funds

  (3) Support for regional revitalization
  - Dispatch of experts to regional financial institutions
  - Dispatch of experts and capital injection for regional revitalization funds

Fig. 7 Outline of the Regional Economy Vitalization Corporation of Japan. (Source: Financial Services Agency, Japan)

improvements and turnarounds. From this perspective, the FSA's supervisory policy for the current fiscal year sees this year as an important period for financial institutions to initiate full-fledged support to help SMEs improve their business operations and strengthen business structures. To this end, we are going to examine whether financial institutions provide appropriate advice to SMEs, not just in financial aspects but also in terms of other management challenges, such as how to boost sales increases. We will examine whether financial institutions help customers to improve their business operations and strengthen their business structures by providing advice for boosting sales in cooperation with outside organizations and experts.

To support initiatives for business improvements and turnarounds of firms, the Regional Economy Vitalization Corporation of Japan was established through public and private investment (Fig. 7). This corporation was originally established to support the business turnaround of companies in the regions. The law relating to the corporation was amended in March 2013, and the corporation can now provide funds, human resources, and know-how to financial institutions and investment funds to help them support business turnarounds and the revitalization of regional economies.

Furthermore, regional financial institutions also need to make efforts to increase new loans and implement measures for improving the business of customer firms through innovative ideas. The FSA has compiled a casebook of pioneering initiatives in these areas. The casebook covers initiatives taken by financial institutions across Japan in four areas of financial institutions' challenges. The areas are providing new loans, improving profits from core business, supporting customer firms' business improvement and business turnaround, and providing support for initiating business. It is very important for financial institutions to consider their customer firms' problems as their own and work hard with them. The purpose of this casebook is to promote such efforts.

In concluding my presentation, I would like to emphasize that regional financial institutions need to draw up medium- to long-term management strategies for the next five to 10 years, as deposits are expected to start decreasing in the regional areas. It is also important that the FSA and the management of regional financial institutions discuss and examine the sustainability of the business models of regional financial institutions. Regional financial institutions live and progress with their respective regions. Therefore, regional financial institutions must improve their institutional framework and foster human resources in order to support the business turnaround and improvement of regional SMEs, revitalize regional economies, and promote new industries in the region.

Session 2: Finance to SMEs through Banks, Capital Markets, and Other Financial Methods

Suhaedi, Ganeshan Wignaraja, Jongsoon Shin, Wako Watanabe, Yoshiaki Ogura, Salinee Wangtal, and Hisashi Ono

Address by Session Chair

Suhaedi

Good afternoon, ladies and gentlemen. My name is Suhaedi, Executive Director of Bank Indonesia Regional Office covering Sulawesi, Maluku, and the Papua Islands. Firstly, I would like to thank the Japanese FSA, ADBI, and the IMF for their invitation. It is a great pleasure and honor to chair this very important session, the focus of which is finance to SMEs, with prominent speakers and commentators. As you may be aware, the topics of finance to SMEs, as well as financial inclusion, have become popular topics and are discussed everywhere. It seems to me, this is a kind of paradox because of two things. SMEs have a significant role in economic development, both in the developed and the developing economies.

Suhaedi
Bank Indonesia Regional Office for Eastern Indonesia, Surabaya, Indonesia

G. Wignaraja
Asian Development Bank Institute, Tokyo, Japan

J. Shin
International Monetary Fund, Tokyo, Japan

W. Watanabe
Faculty of Business and Commerce, Keio University, Tokyo, Japan

Y. Ogura
School of Political Science and Economics, Waseda University, Tokyo, Japan

S. Wangtal
Supervision Group, Bank of Thailand, Bangkok, Thailand

H. Ono
Deputy Director-General, Supervisory Bureau, Financial Services Agency, Tokyo, Japan

ADB Institute, Financial Services Agency, Japan, International Monetary Fund Regional Office for Asia and the Pacific (eds.), *Financial System Stability, Regulation, and Financial Inclusion,* ADB Institute Series on Development Economics, DOI 10.1007/978-4-431-55254-3_4

They make up about 90% of the enterprises in the world and account for more than 50% of employment. They also play an important role in generating employment and alleviating poverty. But we also see that the development of SMEs is still constrained by limited access to finance, their small size, lack of credit ratings, and also by problems with collaterals that make it difficult to get access to finance. So raising the level of SME financing is crucial to promoting growth as well as promoting jobs and alleviating poverty.

Is Finance a Binding Constraint for SME Participation in Trade?

Ganeshan Wignaraja

SMEs are clearly a very important part of Asia's economy. In this presentation, I am going to explore the issues with respect to international trade and look at the People's Republic of China (PRC) and Association of Southeast Asian Nations (ASEAN) countries, and at 8000 companies across these countries. This is a work in progress and a paper exists (Jinjarak et al. 2014).

Essentially, I am going to do five things in the brief time available. I will talk a bit about the context and outline of the study. Then I shall discuss the theory underlying the paper. And then I am going to discuss a little about the macro trends relating to finance, SMEs, and trade. Then I am going to discuss a little about the firm-level econometric results. Finally, I will conclude.

In terms of the context for this, as we saw in the first panel this morning, we had the great collapse of the world economy and also the Asian economy in the post-global-financial crisis era, and trade also had collapsed after that point. That really showed us the importance of the finance–trade link. Trade finance in particular was a major issue in that crisis. Since 2008, we have had a recovery in trade and in growth to some extent. Part of it is due to a lot of fiscal and monetary stimulus that has occurred, and Asia is exporting its way to growth. But we are not really sure what is happening to firms in this whole story. We thought we would look at this because it is so important for inclusive growth.

When people think of inclusive growth, they normally think of education and health as very important parts of the growth story. But we also think that SMEs are very important as a vehicle to create jobs and therefore ensure more participation of the poor in such development. Essentially, what we try to do is to build on the existing theory, and to draw on different fields, which I will give you a taste of, both trade and industrial organization, as well as finance. What this literature emphasizes is that firms differ. Some firms are better than others in terms of being able to participate in trade, as well as business activity. We want to analyze what are the characteristics of firms that do better than others in terms of trading and whether size is a factor in this game, and what role finance plays.

So we are trying to examine different relationships. One is what are the characteristics of firms that trade, and how does finance play a role in this, and what are the other characteristics of firms that come into play? Is it just size or are there other things in play? We have this dataset from the World Bank Enterprise Survey, which has a large number of economies, and we selected the PRC and some ASEAN countries. The total Asian sample covers a multitude of sectors in some 8000 randomly selected firms. So we have an interesting story to tell and a lot of this data is from 2011 surveys, making this a very recent picture.

Many of you are familiar with the theory. There are many channels through which finance plays a role in terms of business activity, and there is this very interesting paper by King and Levine, which you can look at. Of course, trade and finance also come into play and people like Richard Baldwin have done some very interesting work on this in terms of the Global Financial Crisis. Credit conditions, which were tightened during the crisis, may have discouraged many possible trade transactions.

Now, we think it is not just a one-way relationship; there are actually two-way feedbacks. So trading also helps access to finance and that is part of our story from the macro point of view. Exports determine which industries in a country need more working capital.

More pertinent for the paper is the microeconomic literature that we will be putting to the test. We will be looking at people like Melitz, who first identified that some firms trade better than others. He looked at the characteristics of this and related this to some costs. He came up with the conclusion that only the really productive firms were able to export. That notion has been tested by others, including Jensen and Bellone, and that extends this idea to productivity also being linked to finance and access to finance being important.

Then there is related literature coming from Neo-Heckscher–Ohlin models, as well as theories of technology and trade that suggest that there are other factors that are also important when it comes to looking at trade, apart from productivity and finance. Foreign ownership for instance is important, as are skills, technology, and so on. So the differentiated firm that gets into exports is not only productive but needs finance, and has all these other characteristics associated with it. So scale and firm size matter. We tried to test this using econometric analysis.

So coming back to firm size and exports and the theory in general, people assume that large firms are the more competitive ones compared to SMEs in exports because large firms have more resources to meet the fixed costs of exporting and they also have scale economies. The same literature assumes, parallel-wise, that SMEs are at a disadvantage because they lack the resources and networks needed to trade, and they suffer disproportionately from market imperfections and regulations. SMEs are also likely to be disproportionately affected by financial crises and economic downturns including being deprived of access to credit.

Now what we test in the modeling is essentially a set of regressions with two-way relationships. One is export participation linked to various characteristics, size, and other variables. Then we do these seemingly unrelated regressions to try to see what the interrelationships between these variables are.

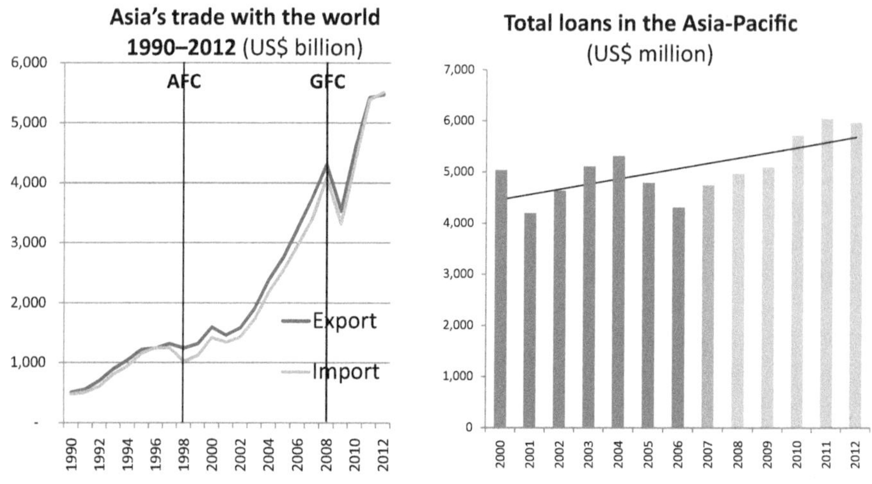

Fig. 1 Macro trends—finance, trade, and small and medium-sized enterprises

Here is a brief picture of the macro story that builds on this trade finance link, linked to the Global Financial Crisis (Fig. 1). The chart on the left-hand side (Asia's trade with the world) shows you the story of the great trade collapse and the recovery. We are little bit uncertain where this will go in the future, which is why the line at the top is getting a bit flat.

As the right hand side chart displaying total loans in Asia indicates, this is clearly linked to a massive increase in financing that has occurred in the region. You get some picture of this with the trend line upwards and this is what shows up in Asia. Now the interesting question is the size issue in all of this. When we come to size, we have talked a lot about SMEs and these two charts below (Fig. 2) give you a sense of SMEs in the PRC and the ASEAN countries, both in terms of their share of employment and their contribution to GDP.

The data suggest that SMEs are very important in economic activity in Asian countries, particularly in employment, but also somewhat important in GDP. But, of course, the countries differ because of the ways in which SMEs are represented in the industrial structure. Also, in part, the definitions of what is an SME vary between these countries. While SMEs are important in economic activity, they are less important in trade in ASEAN countries. Interestingly, the PRC has relatively high SME export shares.

We are trying to get estimates before and after the crisis to try to amplify this picture. But the general conclusion is that, applying the most recent estimates, SMEs have not been that important in trade of Asian countries.

There are many factors that affect why firms actually do business, and here are some of the things that SMEs talk about. If you look at all the country figures, one factor that they have perceived to be a big issue is deficit of trust (Table 1). SMEs mention anti-competitive behavior being a big constraint on the way that they expand. But the second most important factor is finance. This is very interesting,

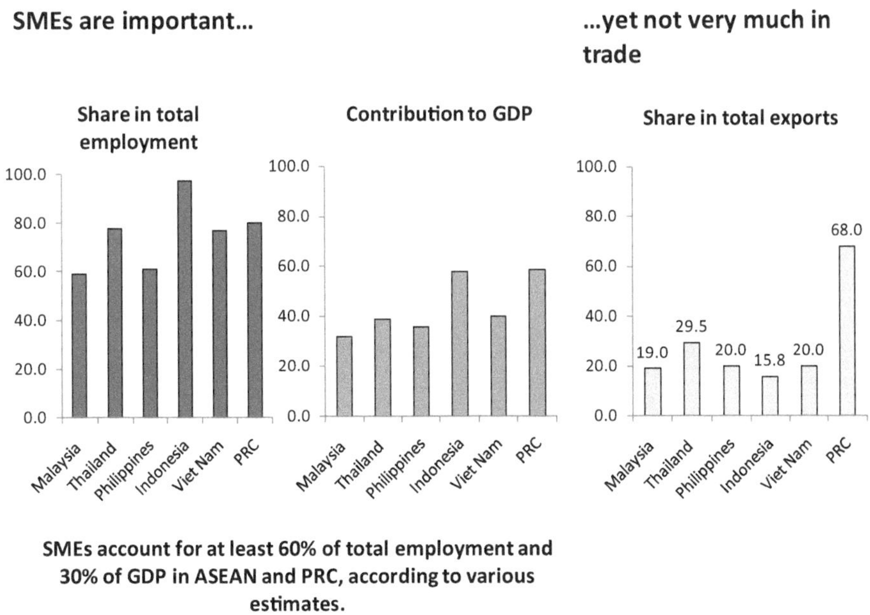

Fig. 2 Share of small and medium-sized enterprises in total employment, contribution to gross domestic product, and total exports. *ASEAN* Association of Southeast Asian Nations, *GDP* gross domestic product, *PRC* People's Republic of China, *SMEs* small and medium-sized enterprises. (Source: Various statistical agencies (ASEAN SME data, Business in Asia, Department of Trade and Industry Philippines, PRC Ministry of Industry and Information Technology))

Table 1 Impact of business environment on small and medium-sized enterprises. Perceived major obstacles to conducting business (% of small and medium-sized firms). (Source: World Bank, Enterprise Survey (various years))

	All countries	Malaysia	Thailand	Philippines	Indonesia	Viet Nam
Major obstacles	Trust deficit (39%)	Tax rates (31%)	Skills gap (60%)	Trust deficit (45%)	Access to credit (39%)	Access to credit (39%)
	Access to credit (35%)	Crime etc. (25%)	Trust deficit (56%)	Tax rates (43%)	Trust deficit (37%)	Trust deficit (35%)
	Electricity (30%)	Skills gap (24%)	Tax rates (55%)	Electricity (37%)	Electricity (31%)	Access to land (25%)

"Other" obstacles—trust deficit hampers intra-firm cooperation; smuggling also a disincentive
Supply-side factors—Lack of access to finance; inadequate worker skills; high electricity costs; poor transport systems
Policy incentives—high corporate tax rates; economic uncertainty; cumbersome customs and corruption

Table 2 Finance is an Asian small and medium-sized enterprise concern. (Source: International Finance Corporation 2011. Enterprise Finance Gap Database)

	Total credit gap	Credit gap per SME
PRC	US$ 62.73 billion	US$ 262,048
Thailand	US$ 11.83 billion	US$ 758,737
Indonesia	US$ 11.77 billion	US$ 172,479
Malaysia	US$ 7.96 billion	US$ 757,412
Viet Nam	US$ 4.28 billion	US$ 253,296
Philippines	US$ 2.03 billion	US$ 356,207

"Credit gap" is the difference between formal credit provided to SMEs and total estimated potential need for formal credit based on McKinsey & Co. estimates

because most surveys talk about finance being the number one factor. So SME finance is important, but it is not necessarily always the most important constraint across different countries. Another way of picking up this macro story is data from the International Finance Corporation (IFC) that try to capture what they call the credit gap, which is the difference between the formal credit provided to SMEs and SMEs' total estimated potential need of formal credit. The IFC data indicates 8 million SMEs in Asia and the Pacific do not have sufficient access to finance according to how the IFC estimates this. That number is very interesting when it is compared to other regions. Thus, Asia has the largest number of SMEs globally that appear not to have sufficient access to finance.

Table 2 provides data on the total credit gap and the credit gap per SME in the PRC and ASEAN countries. The credit gap per SME is larger in more developed ASEAN countries like that in Thailand and Malaysia than others. This partly reflects credit needs at different levels of development. So this is to give you a sense of the credit gap and the interrelationships, and this is all quite recent data. It shows that finance appears to be a big macro concern, but this is as far as the macro story can take us. Starting to get to the firm-level results, here is a simple chart (Fig. 3) that gives you the percentage of firms by different firm size categories that rely on bank loans for about 25 % of their working capital. Strikingly, about 76 % of all SMEs in our Asian sample of 8000 firms rely on bank loans for about 25 % of their working capital. The number falls as the firms get larger.

It is a general problem of access to bank credit, but it is highest for the SME section. It varies by country. Of course, in Thailand and Malaysia the numbers are a bit different, and that may be also because they are more developed than others and have perhaps more open capital markets and better industrial structures than these other countries.

Looking at the econometric exercise, we tried to model what drives trade and we looked at the issue of finance as well as size, and then we looked at the interrelationships between these variables. Let me briefly mention the results before I jump to the conclusions. So here is one set of indicators, and what you find is that the SME indicator is negatively correlated with trading performance measured by exports to sales ratios. So SMEs suffer or have less in trade compared to large firms (Table 3).

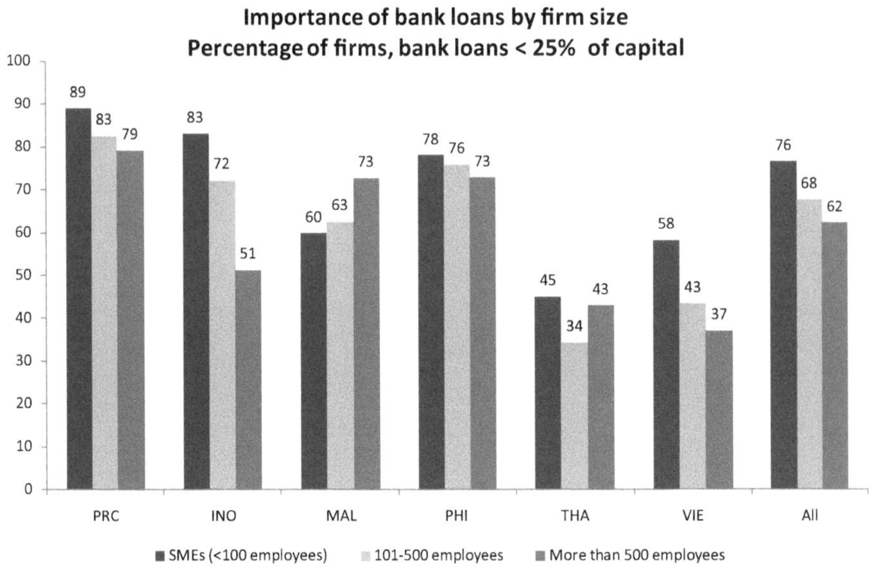

Fig. 3 Firm-level microeconometric results. Columns represent percentages of category-classified, national samples. (Source: Author's calculations on World Bank Enterprise survey data)

Bank borrowing and trade credit are obviously positively correlated with trading. Other factors also affect trading when we get to the other set of relationships. The other factors that come into play are foreign ownership and skills as well as finance. So we get both-way relationships that are important.

Let me conclude. Essentially, we find it is very useful to combine macro data with micro data when it comes to studying this issue of trade and finance, particularly after the financial crisis. Essentially, the trade recovery we think is linked to the importance of understanding different strengths and resilience in Asia's industrial structure. When we break up the PRC and ASEAN countries, which are very important in the trade recovery because they are the bulk traders in Asia, we find that financial development really matters crucially for trade.

SMEs are very important in economic activity, but not so much in trade, and a lack of credit is a major constraint for SMEs, particularly when it comes to exporting behavior. The firm-level results confirm this interesting finding. We also find that this two-way relationship with exporting is positively related to finance. So the medium-sized firms are an interesting area for us to study in the future, because being very small is a big disadvantage in trading and also in attracting access to finance.

Our analysis throws four fascinating policy questions. The first question is this missing middle. People talk a lot about the medium end of firms, firms perhaps between 100 employees and maybe up to 200, or measured in another way between 50 and 100 employees again depending on the definition. Are medium-sized firms a driver of both exporting as well as accessing finance? We shall explore this further in our research.

Table 3 Baseline export function estimates and expanded estimates. (Source: Authors' estimates)

A. Baseline export function estimates

	PRC	ASEAN	PRC + ASEAN, by industry type		
			Labor-intensive	Capital-intensive	Services
SME indicator	-31.04*** (4.61)	-104.16*** (3.73)	-131.04*** (7.24)	-76.20*** (4.03)	-74.90** (29.41)
Age	0.17 (0.26)	-0.50*** (0.14)	-0.77*** (0.25)	-0.73*** (0.16)	0.01 (0.91)
Bank borrowing	0.43*** (0.14)	0.20*** (0.05)	0.33*** (0.09)	0.00 (0.06)	0.70* (0.38)
Non-bank borrowing	-0.27 (0.41)	0.37* (0.21)	0.39 (0.41)	0.50** (0.24)	-5.77 (7.25)
Trade credit	0.66*** (0.19)	0.26*** (0.08)	0.40*** (0.15)	0.10 (0.09)	-0.08 (0.61)
Constant	-45.39*** (6.12)	41.50*** (4.41)	67.59*** (8.02)	49.43*** (5.15)	-178.49*** (44.15)
Observations	2,523	5,557	1,808	2,901	848

Dependent variable: Share of exports in firm sales (0%–100%)

B. Expanded estimates.Estimates with firm-level controls do not change results

	PROBIT	OLS	TOBIT		SUR
SME indicator	-0.90*** (0.03)	-21.54*** (0.88)	N.A.	Firm size (employment)	0.24*** (0.01)
Age	-0.02 (0.02)	-2.90*** (0.37)	-3.33** (1.42)	Age	-0.01 (0.01)
Bank borrowing	0.05*** (0.02)	0.05 (0.41)	3.77*** (1.31)	External finance indicator	0.003*** (0.00)
Non-bank borrowing	0.02 (0.02)	0.01 (0.30)	0.45 (1.33)	Foreign ownership	0.73*** (0.03)
Trade credit	(0.05)*** (0.02)	0.26 (0.39)	2.73** (1.29)	Foreign license	-0.20 (0.16)
Firm size (employment)	N.A.	N.A.	14.99*** (1.20)	Patent ownership	-0.19 (0.24)
Firm size x external finance interactions	N.A.	N.A.	Yes	Worker education	0.16*** (0.04)
Industry & Country FE	Yes	Yes	Yes	Financial certification	0.03 (0.02)
Observations	8,080	8,080	8,080	Observations	8,080

Dependent variable: Share of exports in firm sales (0%–100%).

The second question is what role should central banks and financial supervision agencies really play in looking at credit allocation, particularly for financial inclusion, and how far should this go? Should it really move toward directed credit or should we be talking about the most market-based system with some elements of self-selection? The third important question relates to financial targeting, and should we consider targeting geographies where we know there are vulnerable entrepreneurs as well as firms? Should we be looking at gender issues in this game, etc.?

The last point I think that was important from this whole discussion is what complementary policies of non-finance support should we be considering? Finance is very important, but there are many other things, (such as technical efficiency, R&D, skill creation and attracting foreign investment) which influence the trading activity of firms. Perhaps we should best consider the issues of SME finance and business support in the context of entry into global value chains.

Thank you very much.

Finance to Small and Medium-Sized Enterprises in Japan and Asia[1]

Jongsoon Shin

Good afternoon, ladies and gentlemen. It is my pleasure to give a presentation on SME financing in Japan and Asia. In my presentation, I will briefly touch upon the contribution of SMEs to an economy and their challenges. Against this backdrop, I will go over credit information issues and the design of risk sharing, particularly in credit guarantee schemes.

In Asia, SMEs contribute a sizable share to GDP and employment. In advanced economies, SMEs account for about 50 % of GDP and in low-income countries it is about 30 %. Also, on average SMEs represent around 70 % of total employment in the region. More generally, SMEs create a greater share of jobs than larger firms. However, it should be noted that not all small firms are growth-friendly. According to Mazzucato (2013), the firms that are most important to growth are the small number of fast-growing firms that create the greatest employment increase.

In other words, not all small firms are high-growth but many high-growth firms are small. Despite the significance of SMEs, they face tough challenges (Fig. 4). For example in Japan, the profitability of SMEs has declined over the last few decades. Also, compared with the other advanced economies, return on assets of smaller firms remains low at around 2 %, which is far below the average of 8 % in other advanced economies.

---

[1] The views expressed in this presentation are those of the author and should not be reported as or attributed to the International Monetary Fund, its Executive Board, or the governments of any of its members.

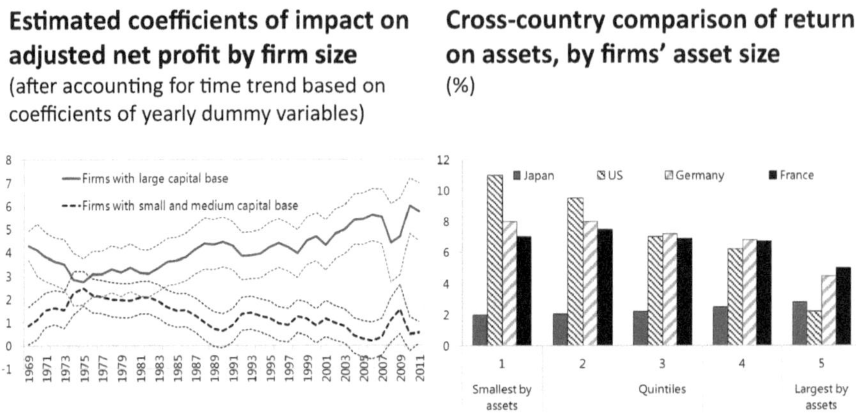

Fig. 4 Challenges to small and medium-sized enterprises: low profitability. Source: Lam and Shin 2012. *Left,* Notes: (1) Firms with large capital base refer to firms with capital of ¥ 1 billion or more, while firms with medium capital base have between ¥ 100 million and ¥ 1000 million yen and between ¥ 10 million and ¥ 100 million for firms with small capital base. See Ministry of Finance (MOF) for definition. (2) *Dotted lines* refer to standard errors of the estimated coefficients. (Source: Authors' estimates based on MOF data). *Right* (Source: Tokuda 2011)

In addition, SMEs face challenges in access to finance. In East Asia and South Asia, access to finance has been cited as one of the top three obstacles to growth. Also, it is estimated that around 50 to 60 % of SMEs are under-served. Challenges to SMEs can be broken down into three angles. SMEs contain higher credit risks, but at the same time they lack track records of high-risk credit history. Also, SMEs often are unable to provide adequate collateral to secure bank loans.

From a bank perspective, SME lending means higher transactional costs or higher monitoring costs despite the small size of loans. In terms of access to finance, Asian economies show different levels of access—different degrees of ease of access. According to the World Bank's Doing Business Report, Malaysia ranks the highest out of 185 countries, whereas the Philippines and Indonesia rank low. The evaluation criteria of the chart in the reports consisted of two elements. First, the availability of credit information, second the adoption of movable collateral laws. These two are closely associated with the topics I will discuss.

Credit bureaus play a key or a central role in the financial system (Fig. 5). Credit bureaus enable members to more accurately assess repayment capacity of borrowers and reduce asymmetric information between lenders and borrowers. Therefore, there is a positive correlation between credit information availability and loan availability.

In Asia, credit bureaus are strong in Japan, whereas in the Philippines they are still weak. In the case of Japan, the Credit Risk Database (CRD) is a key part of the financial infrastructure. Its membership consists of more than 180 financial institutions such as banks, and the banks determine the credit ratings of SMEs based on the CRD data. In order to further enhance the credit information infrastructure efforts should be made on three fronts.

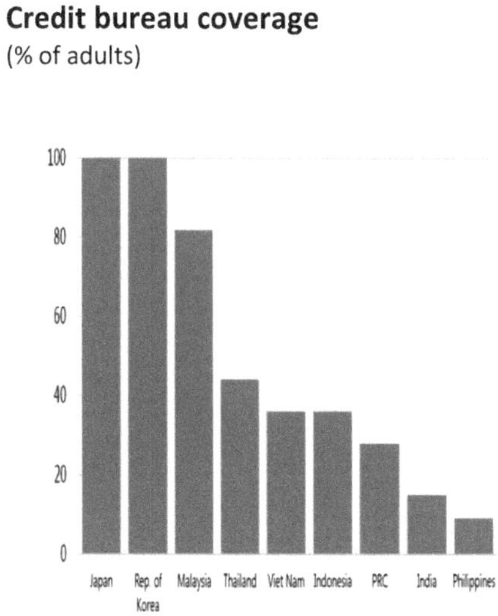

- Japan: Credit Risk Database (CRD)
- Republic of Korea: Korea Credit Bureau (KCB) and National Information and Credit Evaluation (NICE)
- Malaysia: mandatory participation
- Thailand: two credit agencies.
- Indonesia: The Credit Information Bureau was created by Bank Indonesia. Plans to create a private one.
- People's Republic of China: The central bank established the Personal Credit Information Center (PCIC).
- India: Many credit bureaus, but the Credit Information Bureau (India) Limited (CIBIL) is the most important.

Fig. 5 Credit bureaus in Asia. *Left,* Note: The figures for Viet Nam and the PRC are those of their public credit bureaus. (Sources: World Development Index and International Monetary Fund staff calculations). *Right* (Source: Standard Chartered 2013)

First, expand coverage of data and provide more timely data. Second, credit bureaus need to be able to access non-financial information such as utility payments. Third, in doing so, coordination among authorities and institutions is critical. Another key issue in SME finance is the design of risk sharing between vendors and borrowers and between the public and private sectors. Having this in mind, I will discuss credit guarantee schemes.

On the credit guarantee scheme, in the case of an SME default, a government affiliated financial institutions reimburses a pre-determined share of a credit loss. By bearing the brunt of a potential credit loss, governments prompt banks to continue to provide loans to SMEs. Credit guarantees become more important during a crisis when property prices fall sharply and the value of collateral suffers correspondingly. SMEs that mostly rely on real estate as collateral experience additional financial difficulties because the reduced value of the collateral makes it hard for them to meet a bank's lending standards. In this context, governments provide credit guarantees and ease financial conditions. In Japan, the amount of outstanding credit guarantees surged following the crisis.

Asian governments provide highly supportive credit guarantees in terms of the large amount of credit guarantees and the high coverage ratios. In Japan, the outstanding amount of credit guarantees is more than 7%—of GDP. In fact, in Japan more than one third of all SMEs are supported by credit guarantees. The average amount of credit guarantees in Asia is much higher than other regions (Fig. 6).

Coverage ratio is also high in Asia compared with other regions (Fig. 7). According to Beck, Klapper, and Mendoza (2008), the median value of coverage ratios

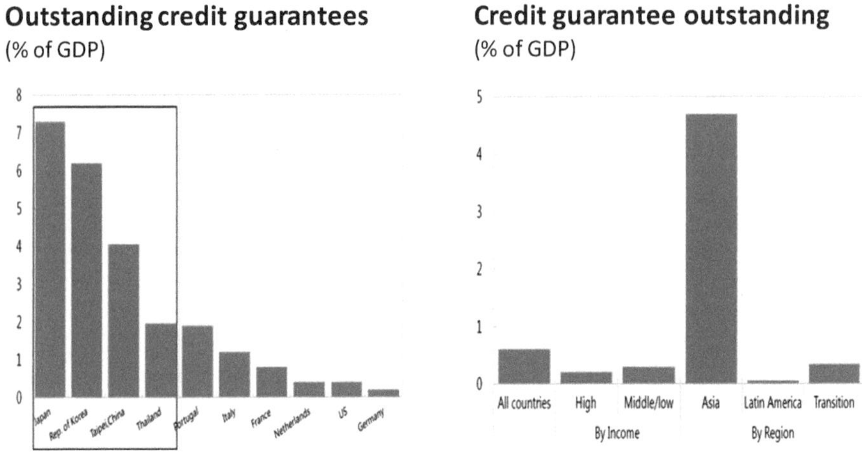

Fig. 6 Outstanding credit guarantees in Asia. *Left*, Notes: United States (2010), Thailand (Q3 2013), other economies (2011). (Source: Organisation for Economic Co-operation and Development 2013). *Right* (Source: Beck et al. 2008)

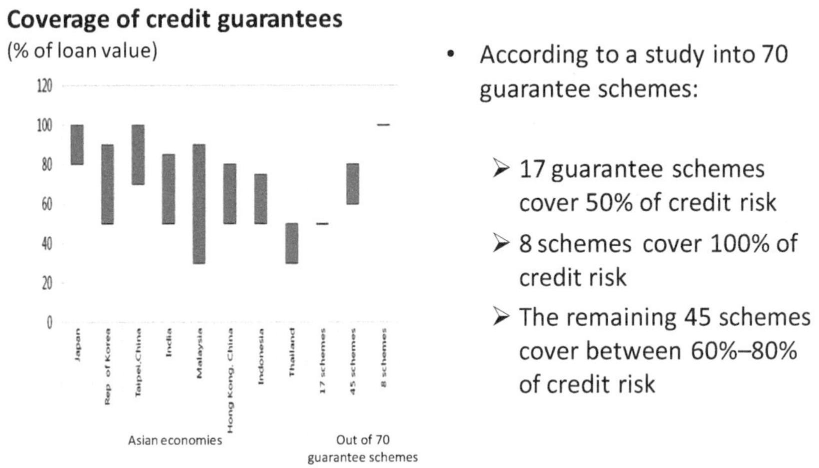

Fig. 7 Coverage of credit guarantees in Asia. *Left* (Sources: Organisation for Economic Co-operation and Development 2013; Japan Ministry of Economy, Trade and Industry; India Credit Guarantee Fund Trust for Micro and Small Enterprises; and International Monetary Fund staff calculations). *Right* (Source: KPMG 2011)

around the world is around 80 %. In contrast, Asian governments provide somewhat more generous coverage ratios. Despite the benefits of credit guarantees, they come at a price. To illustrate this, I will explain the financial conditions of Japanese SMEs following the Global Financial Crisis (Fig. 8).

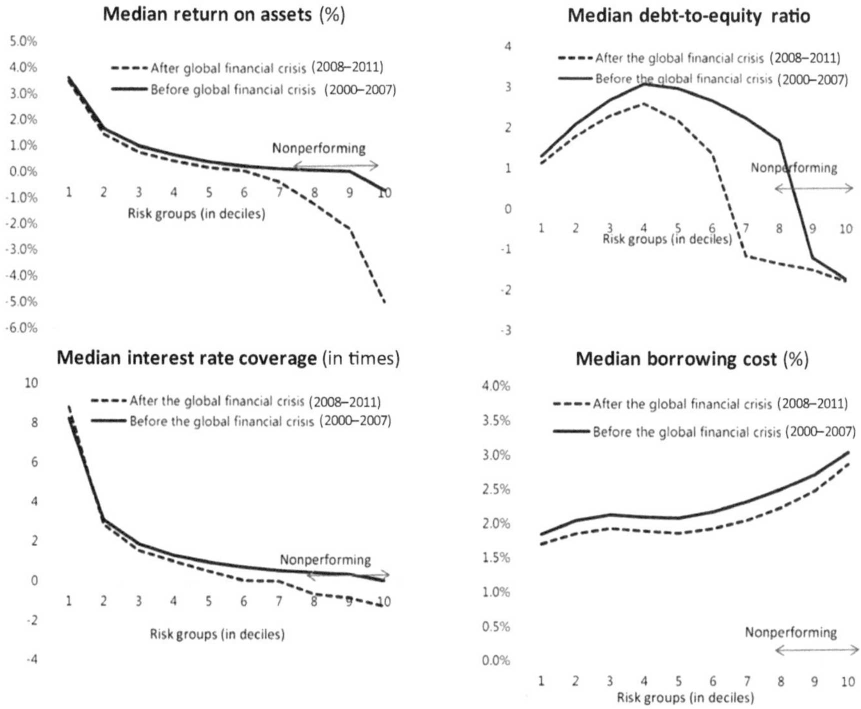

Fig. 8 Impact of generous supportive measures: performance of Japanese small and medium-sized enterprises. (Source: Lam and Shin 2012)

The groups 1–3 represent the strongest SMEs, whereas groups 8–10 represent the weakest SMEs. The solid black line represents before the financial crisis and the red dotted line after the Global Financial Crisis. As you can see, the conditions of the weakest SMEs rose materially after the Global Financial Crisis. Their return on assets declined sharply, the debt-to-equity ratio turned negative. The interest rate coverage ratio also fell below 0. However, these worsening conditions of SMEs, the weak SMEs, did not translate into a rise in their borrowing rates. As you can see in this chart, the bulk of SMEs' borrowing rate declined across all the groups by a similar magnitude.

Also, the spread between the weaker SMEs and the strong SMEs is just around 100 basis points. This is puzzling given the worsened conditions of SMEs. If lenders had fully incorporated the increased level of credit risk in weak SMEs, their lending rates or a firm's borrowing rate should have risen. One explanation could be that the government's crisis measures, such as credit guarantees, helped to ease financial conditions of weak SMEs.

I will explain it from a slightly different angle. The black dotted line is banks' breakeven rate, whereas the gray dashed line represents the actual borrowing rates of banks actual lending rates (Fig. 9). The gap between the two lines implies in price terms that the credit risks must have been borne somewhere outside the banking

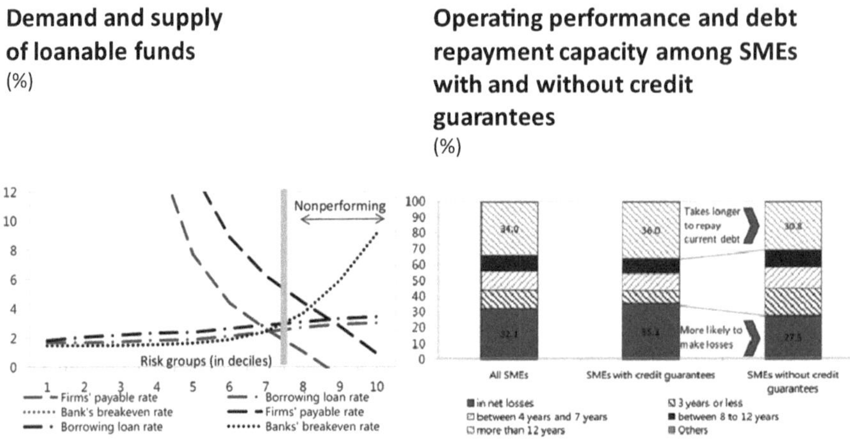

Fig. 9 Impact of generous supportive measures: favorable borrowing rates. (Source: Lam and Shin 2012). *Left,* Note: Gray lines indicate FY2009–2010, while black lines indicate FY2000. *Right, SMEs* small and medium-sized enterprises. Note: Repayment capacity is measured in terms of number of years, which is the ratio of all long- and short-term debts divided by the sum of net income and depreciation expenses. SMEs in operating losses or longer years have weaker repayment capacity on debts. (Source: Japan Credit Risk Database)

sector, such as the public sector, through the credit guarantees or special loans from the government. It is also notable that in the right-hand chart SMEs with credit guarantees are more likely to incur a loss and take more time to repay loans.

Having said that, credit guarantees come at a price. On the one hand, credit guarantees may weaken the risk assessment of the banks and the banks may understate underlying credit risks. On the other hand, credit guarantees may prevent non-viable firms from exiting or being restructured. Therefore, credit guarantees could lead to misallocation of resources and undermine the healthy dynamics of SMEs. Then the question arises, how can we reduce over-reliance on credit guarantees while ensuring smooth access to finance?

One key answer lies in broadening the range of collateral. However, there are major challenges in this regard. Intangible assets such as intellectual property rights are still not eligible for collateral in many countries. Also, small banks find it difficult to determine a fair value for certain types of collateral, such as vendor inventory or current assets. Evidence suggests that a registry of forms such as the introduction of moveable collateral can greatly spur access to finance. In view of this, efforts should be made to establish property registers or improve bankruptcy procedures.

When it comes to funding for innovative tech start-ups, the traditional banking sector, which I have discussed so far, is not perfectly suitable because of the higher level of risk of loss and the long-term investment horizon. Therefore, equity financing for such venture capital plays a main role in this type of funding and policy efforts should be made in this regard.

In conclusion, governments play a key role in facilitating financial intermediation. But policy efforts should be targeted because piling policy upon policy to support SMEs comes with economic costs. Our policy recommendations are: First, to continue to improve the credit information infrastructure. Second, to reduce excessive intervention in credit guarantees, but at the same time broaden the range of collateral. And last but not least, to promote risk capital.

Thank you.

Comments to Session 2

Wako Watanabe

I am very honored to have this opportunity to raise some discussion points. My discussion will be based on a paper published in the Public Policy Review of the Ministry of Finance. I have two co-authors: Professor Ogura, who will make his comments following my comments, and Professor Tadanobu Nemoto.

This is a picture that depicts the structure of the relationship of lending. There are a bank and its borrower, an SME. Organizationally speaking, the bank is divided into two parts: the headquarters and its branch. The bank establishes the relationship with its borrower at its branch. By building the relationship, the bank's branch can collect information from the firm. The information is received by either a branch manager or a loan officer assigned to the firm. There are two types of information: hard information and soft information. Hard information is information such as financial statements and soft information is information that is not quantifiable. The bank's manager can also collect soft information and hard information from the loan officer, because they can make contacts between the two.

However, since the branch and the headquarters are located apart, the contact between the headquarters and the branch is difficult and the soft information collected by the branch cannot be transmitted to headquarters. Only the hard information travels to the headquarters. This is because handling soft information is difficult. Therefore, we can suspect that a more decentralized bank has a greater incentive to collect soft information because soft information is more widely utilized in making decisions.

Formally, we were able to summarize the following discussion into the following proposition of Stein in his paper published in 2002. The proposition is that loan officers put more effort into collecting soft information and the soft information is more greatly utilized at decentralized banks than at centralized banks. In order to test this proposition, we will take the following approach empirically. We conducted a survey of banks about loan decisions. More precisely, we are going to run the following regression: SOFT is a measure for use of soft information and DECENTRAL is a set of measures for decentralized decision-making structure within a bank. We conducted our own survey and the survey we used in our regressions is the Survey on the Realities of and Challenges toward Smoothing Loans to Small and Medium Enterprises. This was conducted by the Research Institute for Economy, Trade and Industry in November 2010. The survey was distributed to all city, regional, regional

2, and Shinkin banks, as well as the credit associations of Japan, and 299 banks responded to the survey. The response rate was about 54 %. These are the variables of our regressions. The independent variable is specifically denoted as SOFTIRANY, which is a dummy variable to indicate whether the financial institution used qualitative information or soft information when rating a borrower internally.

This is a list of a set of independent variables we used in running our regressions: BRANCH is a measure for a bank's branch manager's decision authority for the amount of loan (Table 4). BRANCHSHARE, the third variable in this list, is the proportion of loan applications approved at the branch level rather than at the headquarters level. LAYER is the maximum number of decision layers within a bank. Since our independent variable is a dummy variable, in an economics jargon, we used the probit model to test our proposition.

The results are presented in Table 5. BranchAsset is the measure for the decision authority of a branch manager divided by the size of a bank measured by the bank's total assets. This variable's coefficient is positive and weakly significant.

The marginal effect of the variable is positively significant. This suggests that if the decision authority of a branch manager relative to a bank's size is larger, the bank is more likely to utilize soft information when rating its borrower. This concludes my brief presentation. Thank you very much for listening.

Yoshiaki Ogura

Thank you very much for the opportunity to comment here. My comment is mainly about Mr. Shin's presentation about "zombie" lending and economic growth. I totally agree with the argument for the negative correlation between economic growth and zombie lending. But I would like to point out that we have to be very careful about the causality in deriving a policy prescription.

The first possible causality is what is presented by Mr. Shin. Zombie firms crowd out new entrants, and as a result economic growth becomes weak. The second possible causality is as follows. Because people's growth prospect is so weak, the fund demand for growing firms or the fund demand for new entrants is very weak, so as a result the loans to under-performing SMEs remain larger in proportion to total loans.

If the first causality is true, then just reducing the government guarantee program would be a suitable policy to improve economic growth in Japan. But if the second causality would be true, then the more direct and suitable prescription would be to offer more business opportunities, probably through deregulation or further integration with the Asian economy, which is today's growth center.

So given the fact that the Japanese government guarantee program covers not only older, under-performing SMEs, but also younger and growing SMEs, in my comment I dare to argue for the second causality.

The second argument is supported by Fig. 10, depicting the aggregate cash flow of Japanese corporations. For this figure, the gap between operating cash flow, which is the upper curve, and investment cash flow, which is the lower curve, has become wider and wider in the last decade. After the financial crisis, operating cash flow quickly recovered, but investment did not. This figure suggests that Japanese

Table 4 Independent variables of regression independent variables (DECENTRAL). (Source: Authors' estimates)

Variables	Definition	*N*	Mean	S.D.	Min	Max
BRANCH	The upper limit of the size of an unsecured loan to a performing borrower for a branch manager (10,000 JPY)	272	3063	8141	250	65,000
BRAN-CHASSET	BRANCH/total assets	272	0.000075	0.000108	6.40E-07	0.000682
BRANCH-SHARE	Proportion of the number of loan applications that reach the final decision without an approval by HQ	275	0.475	0.227	0.10	0.95
LAYER	Maximum number of decision layers for a loan approval to a performing borrower (HQ and a branch)	292	7.75	2.07	2	14
ASSET	Total assets (March, 2009, million JPY)	299	554,528	970,252	4556	7,401,837

HARDENED, a dummy variable to indicate a bank that records qualitative info. electronically within an entire bank, and bank type dummies are included as control variables

Table 5 Results of probit model estimation (Shinkin banks only). (Source: Authors' estimates)

	Marginal effect	S.D.	Z value	Marginal effect	S.D.	Z value
BRANCHASSET	1061.93	600.06	1.77*	1226.52	673.75	1.82*
BRANCHSHARE	0.1993	0.2111	0.94	0.0923	0.2050	0.45
LAYER	−0.0083	0.0213	−0.39			
LNASSET				0.0263	0.0536	0.49
N	135			138		

Dep. var. = SOFTIRSCORE (Use of qualitative info. by scoring it when determining credit rating)
If the decision authority relative to bank size is larger, the bank is more likely to utilize soft info
* = significant at 10% level.

corporations are very cautious about taking risks. This tendency seems to be even more evident among medium-sized enterprises, but it is not so clear in terms of small businesses.

Like this, at least we can show indirect evidence for the weak demand on the side of the firms. Investments, too, became weaker as a result of this weak demand for growth, as the lending market competition between banks became harsher and harsher in the last decade in Japan. So as a result, the loan margin of every type of bank kept declining in the last decade. In order to tackle this difficulty, many

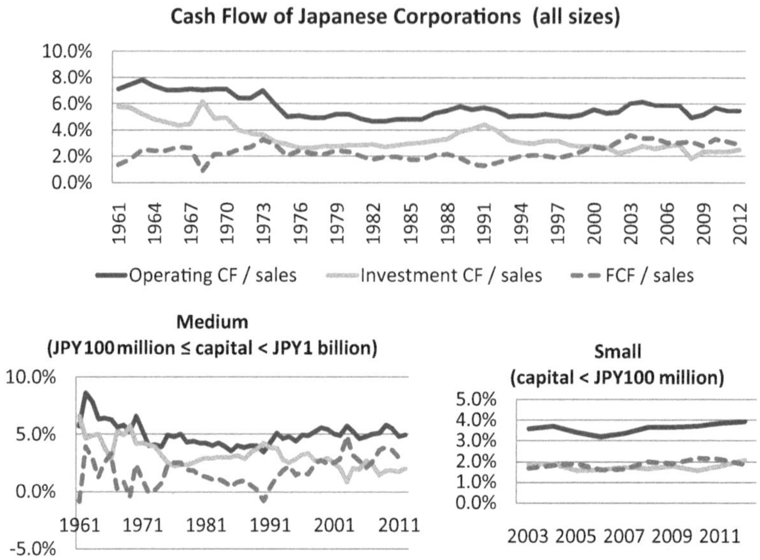

Fig. 10 Weak domestic demand for funds. *CF* cash flow. *Operating CF* equals to (operating profit) + (depreciation)—(annual increase in working capital). *Investment CF* is the sum of the annual investment for tangible assets excluding software and the annual increase in intangible asset. *Free cash flow* (*FCF*) is *operating CF* minus *investment CF*. (Source: Discussant's calculation from the Financial Statements Statistics of Corporations by Industry, Ministry of Finance, Japan)

banks consolidated with each other in the last 15 years (Fig. 11). The consolidations among the major banks seems to be almost finished, and the consolidations among the cooperative banks which include Shinkumi banks and the Shinkin banks are also almost finished (Fig. 12). But the consolidation among regional banks is ongoing.

This wave of bank consolidations could be helpful to improve the credit availability for younger and growing SMEs, by improving the risk-taking ability of the banking sector, and enhancing the incentive for banks to produce customer-specific information. On the other hand, as was mentioned by Professor Watanabe, the complicated decision process after consolidation could deter SME lending, which is more dependent on soft information, which is hard to transmit within an organization. So the problem of the design of decision structures after consolidation could be an important issue in today's Japan.

Thank you.

Salinee Wangtal

Good afternoon, ladies and gentlemen. I would like to thank ADBI for allowing me to be here. I love to be in Japan. It is a very peaceful country compared to where I come from. Actually, I have to say that both papers are very comprehensive, very informative, and very useful. I do not have any comments, except to say that I fully agree. What I agree with is that I think that excessive public support to SMEs, for

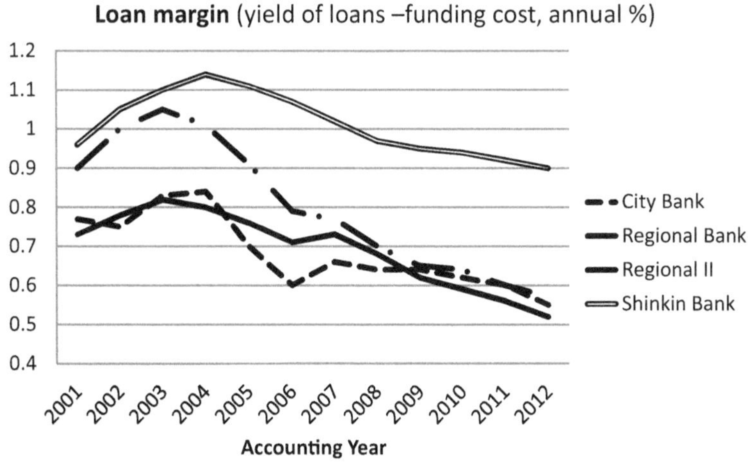

Fig. 11 Lending competition appears to get harsher. (Source: Japanese Bankers Association Website, Shinyou Kinko Gaikyo (Shinkin Central Bank))

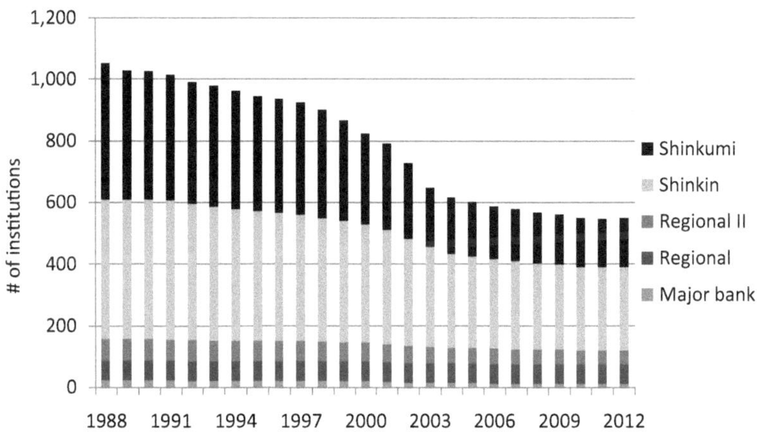

Fig. 12 Bank consolidations. *Major banks* and *cooperative banks*: almost done; *Regional banks*: ongoing. Notes: Figures are for the end of March in each year. Major banks include city banks ("Toshi Ginko"), Shinsei Bank, Aozora Bank, Saitama Risona Bank, and trust banks (excluding trust subsidiaries). (Sources: *Until 2003*: Nikkei Kin'yu Nenpo (Annual Report of the Financial Sector), Nihon Keizai Shinbun Sha. *Since 2003*: *Trust banks*: Trust Companies Association of Japan website, http://www.shintaku-kyokai.or.jp/profile/xls/profile03.xls; *Shinkin banks*: Shinyo Kinko Tokei (Shinkin bank statistics), Shinkin Central Bank Research Institute, http://www.scbri.jp/toukeimokuji.htm; *Shinkumi Banks*: Community Bank Shinyo Kumiai website, http://www.shinyokumiai.or.jp/keisu.html; *Other banks*: Zenkoku Ginko Zaimu Shohyo Bunseki (analysis of national banks financial statements), Japanese Bankers Association, http://www.zenginkyo.or.jp/stats/year2_02/index.html)

a long time, will not benefit them. It will spoil the SMEs. Weak SMEs will survive and they will have to depend on public support forever.

Please be aware that if you want to finish or lift the public support, that this will be somewhat dissatisfactory to the SMEs and may make the authorities unpopular. This is what I have experienced, but I am glad that the SMEs in my country never get excessive support. Actually, the Government of Thailand never supports them. The Thai SMEs will have to struggle on their own. They have to find their own market. They have to find their own bank loan and find everything and try to survive in unpleasant conditions. However, I think this is a blessing in disguise, because it is what makes Thai SMEs strong and able to compete.

In the four or five minutes I have left, I would like to talk to you a little about what is happening to SME financing in Thailand. I will try to compare it to what is described in the paper.

In Thailand, SMEs contribute 40% of the country's GDP (Fig. 13). They get most of their loans from commercial banks and government banks. Recently, what has made us happy is that growth of lending to SMEs has been higher than growth of total bank loans, The green line shows growth of lending to SMEs, which has been 14% higher than growth of total bank loans, depicted by the dotted black line, which is about 10% (Fig. 14). This did not happen because the Thai SMEs are lucky. Rather, I think that it is a result of a combination of several support programs. Lending growth for large corporations, as you can see at the bottom, is only 4%. Large corporations do not want to borrow from banks anymore. They issue their own debentures, which is cheaper, so banks mobilize deposits and then they have funds with which they do not know what to do and then they have to lend to someone. They think that lending to SMEs is more profitable, so they lend to SMEs. This is a fact of life, which I think probably somebody will say is not true, but I will say that it is true.

Even though Thai SMEs have a high lending growth, they still face many obstacles to get bank loans. The most important obstacle is, I would say, a lack of collateral. Because when banks lend to SMEs they cannot estimate the future cash flow. Why can they not do that? Because the financial statements of SMEs, as you can imagine, are not accurate. SMEs usually report lower earnings in order to avoid tax. I do not know if this happens in your country or not, but it happens in Thailand. So banks cannot depend on the financial statements of SMEs and they have to depend just on collateral.

By doing this, the bank will lend 60% of the total value of collateral. So even for high- potential SMEs, there is only a limited chance that they will get a larger bank loan. They have one piece of collateral and for that they get a certain amount of bank loan. They are good in business so they want to expand their business, but they cannot because they already used up their collateral. This is why in Thailand we have a large number of small SMEs, but these small enterprises cannot move up to become medium-sized enterprises.

I will talk to you about the support program. I would say create a guarantee, even though some would say that this is not very good in the long term, but I would say it is still important. Because this helps the SME that do not have collateral. In Thailand

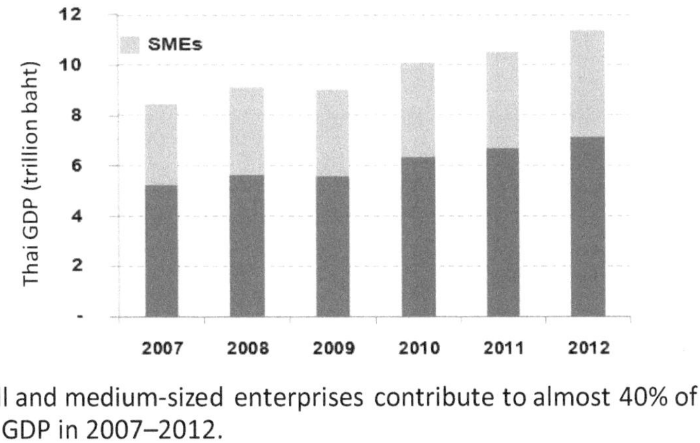

Fig. 13 Significance of small and medium-sized enterprises to Thai economy. *GDP* gross domestic product, *SMEs* small and medium-sized enterprises. (Source: Bank of Thailand)

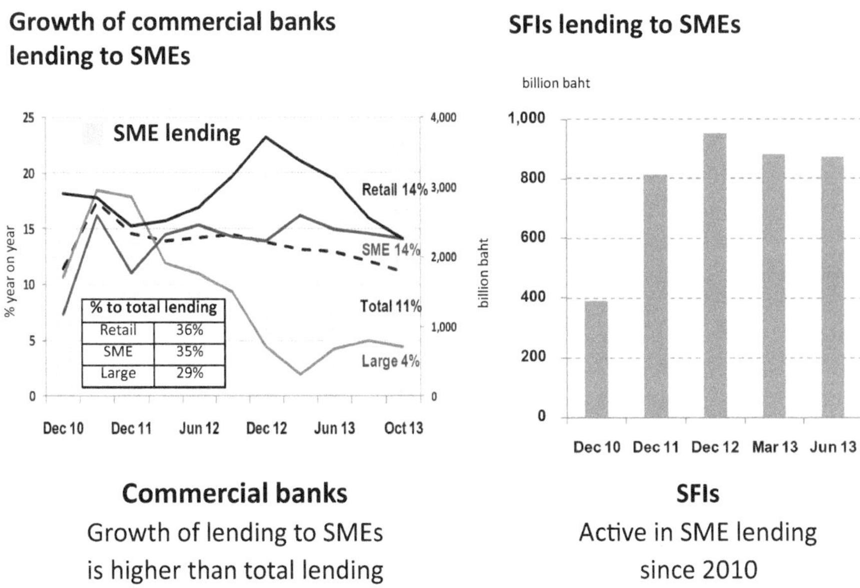

Fig. 14 Banks increase lending to small and medium-sized enterprises. *SFI* specialized financial institution, *SMEs* small and medium-sized enterprises. (Source: Bank of Thailand)

in the past, the credit guarantee was very ineffective because it was too strict. But we changed this during the global crisis to help the SMEs that were affected by it. It has become more flexible and banks have been lending under this guarantee.

Another support program I would like to talk about is trying to set up information centers for SMEs because no matter how much, how large the credit line, it would not be enough. We need to create incentives for banks to lend to SMEs based on their own commercial decisions. So what the Bank of Thailand tried to do is to set up information centers, so that banks can access the centers to analyze the loan applications from SMEs in a shorter time and using fewer resources.

Another issue is that we tried to help push for a new law which is a collateral law. In Thailand, the legal collateral is only land and buildings. The new law that has been enacted will add to the legal collateral things like lease holdings and inventories. Having more intangible assets will help high-potential-growth SMEs.

I would like to conclude by saying that SME financing in Thailand has been improving a lot, but we still need to continue the support program. As for the central bank, what we tried to do is to focus on high-potential SMEs and help them get more bank loans. By doing this, we will not lower the quality of bank lending. As for the Thai government, through the Ministry of Finance, it tries to help micro-SMEs, meaning very small SMEs that now borrow from loan sharks and pay excessively high interest rates. This is true in my country. They would like these micro-SMEs to pay lower interest rates, for example 36 % per annum, or thereabouts.

Let me talk just a bit about financial stability, as I am a Chief Supervisor of the Bank of Thailand. I will say that loans to SMEs, even though they have a higher probability of default—I think you are familiar with the BIS term—it is easier for SMEs to become NPLs, but the loss rate is very low because SME loans are fully collateralized. It is not like large corporates. The probability of default is low, but so is the collateral. So when a large corporate loan becomes bad, it hits the bank seriously. Another good point about the SME sector is that it is diversified. So in Thailand, SME lending never harms the stability of our banking sector.

So these are all my comments. Thank you very much.

Hisashi Ono[2]

I think everybody agrees on the growth potential of SMEs in Asian economies. Actually, SMEs are also very important in the Japanese economy. SMEs account for more than 70 % of total employment in Japan. Especially in local areas, SMEs have large shares of employment, and they play main roles in regional economies.

Therefore, a very important and common theme for Japan and Asian countries is how to support SMEs through various measures, including financial instruments. The Japanese FSA has been making various efforts so that financial institutions, especially regional financial institutions, entirely and adequately support the business of SMEs.

Needless to say, self-efforts by SMEs are indispensable. However, there may be some limitation to what SMEs themselves can do. Financial institutions are expected to provide support for improving the corporate structure and business management of SMEs, because I believe supporting and nurturing SMEs is the basic roles for financial institutions.

[2] The views expressed are those of the author and do not necessarily reflect the views of the Financial Services Agency or the FSA Institute.

FSA is changing the way of financial administration in order to focus on checking the primary roles of financial institutions. As I mentioned, there are two things that are expected for financial institutions. The first is to strengthen support for the improvement of corporate structure and business management. The second is to provide credit and equity-like funds to promote industries in the regions.

To fulfill such expected tasks, regional financial institutions are required to strengthen human resources and know-how, financial foundation, and organization though various reforms. Just as Professor Ogura pointed out, I think these reforms include the implementation of integration, realignment, cooperation, and alliances among different institutions. Needless to say, bank consolidation is not the only solution. However, financial institutions should verify the sustainability of the business model and draw up business strategies.

The second comment is about the collateral and guarantee. As Dr. Shin pointed out, lack of adequate collateral and personal guarantees are major challenges to SME financing. In this respect, the Japanese FSA has been promoting active utilization of asset-based lending, which is lending backed by movable properties and accounts receivable. Collateral for financial institutions is mainly mortgage collateral in Japan, and movable properties and accounts receivable have not been so much utilized as collateral.

However, asset-based lending has merits not only for customer enterprises, but also for financial institutions. For SMEs, through the utilization of movable properties and accounts receivable as collateral, financial facilities will be expanded. For financial institutions, credit risk management will be enhanced because asset-based lending helps financial institutions understand the actual conditions of their customer enterprises.

With regard to personal guarantees, in Japan the guideline regarding personal guarantees were just established last month among the parties including representatives of financial institutions, SMEs, lawyers, and governments. The guideline stipulates the cases, and the conditions under which personal guarantees do not need to be provided and the procedures financial institutions are required to follow when asking client enterprises to provide personal guarantees. This guideline will apply from next month, February. We expect that this guideline for personal guarantees will reduce unnecessary burdens for SMEs.

Finally, as regards the credit guarantee, needless to say, excessive relying on credit guarantees will induce moral hazard for borrowers, that is, losing self-discipline of enterprises while weakening the credit risk assessment of financial institutions. In the past, Japanese credit guarantee schemes covered 100 % of credit risk. However, taking into account the bad effects of full coverage, it was decreased from 100 to 80 % in 2007.

When the global financial shock occurred, the current ratio of guarantee was increased again to 100 % for specific industries that were significantly affected by the shock of the financial crisis. The scope of full coverage of 100 % has been gradually reduced to break out of 100 % guarantees.

This is my comment. Thank you, Mr. Chairman.

Open Floor Discussion

Suhaedi: Thank you very much Mr. Ono. We have been entertained by excellent presentations from speakers and discussants. Before I open the floor for Q&A and comments, it is interesting to note that most speakers and commentators realize the importance of SMEs in financing, and the constraints. Also, they offer solutions in the area of financial policy, maybe because we are coming from financial authorities and financial institutions. We need policies integrated with government policies in the real sectors.

Participant: Thank you very much for your wonderful presentations and also the discussions. I have some comments for Dr. Shin on the finance of SMEs in Japan and Asia, particularly on page 4 where it talks about the credit bureaus in Asia. Dr. Shin mentioned about Japan's CRD. Just to elaborate a little about the CRD, if I may, this was originally started as the credit guarantee corporations in Japan. There are 52 of them and they get together to provide the data in order to have the nationwide average credit risk profile, which is not biased regionally, but is balanced on average across industries and SMEs.

So it is not the banks that originated this credit risk database, but rather the guarantee corporation that is strongly linked to the credit guarantee system in Japan. In that regard, I think what is a most important development in this CRD is the introduction of very low credit guarantee fees, which were introduced a couple of years ago in order to minimize moral hazard and increase the incentives for SMEs, because there used to be uniform credit guarantee fees charged on related good SMEs or bad SMEs. Because we now have a variable fee for credit guarantees, there is an incentive for SMEs to improve their performance, which I think is a very small step, but it is very important in order to minimize moral hazard and other things.

Related to this—and I am coming to my question—as one of the policy implications, Dr. Shin suggested developing credit information and market infrastructure. But there are two distinctly different credit databases. One is the credit bureau, which has the credit histories of individual companies—company A's credit history, company B's credit history, etc. But CRD is an anonymous database, which basically has the representative benchmark for a certain industry by category and such, and probably belongs in the domain of public goods rather than private goods.

The central bank of Thailand is very eager to develop this type of credit risk database, so this is a public goods area. What is the view of Dr. Shin regarding developing this credit information and market infrastructure—should it be developed by the private sector competitively, or should it be done by public organizations or a government-sponsored entity? That is my question, thank you very much.

Jongsoon Shin: Thank you for a great question. First of all, I would like to agree with your points about the importance of variable fees and I am also aware that the structure of the membership in CRD is diverse. Regarding your questions, if you look region-wide, most of the countries have credit bureaus, and what I found was that there is a limitation of credit registry or credit institutions when they are rated by public institutions. For example in the case of the PRC, the central bank introduced a personal credit information center (PCIC), but the public sector itself cannot cover all the information. I think, as we know about the importance of markets, not only the public sector but also private sectors should play a key role in providing credit information to the market players. I think it is not mutually exclusive, or that it is a choice between public and private. It should be provided in both ways.

Experience suggests that, eventually, the private sector such as credit bureaus will play a bigger role in providing credit information. But I think also, as in the case of CRD, that the government or public sector should play a role in the coordination and gather more data and provide more relevant data. So that is my answer.

Participant: A very short topic. My question is whether private or public is because of the proprietorship of the information? It is easy for you to say collect all the information, but no SMEs would like to submit any meaningful credit information to any private entity very easily. There are very famous sayings like Professor Yoshino here always mentions there are four types of balance sheet or the P/L which are distributed to tax authorities, to your wife, or to the authorities and things like that. So, naturally, with proprietorship there is always the following question, which is a bit hard: why do you have to provide the data if it is very disadvantageous to you when your credit history is made available to everybody?

For the banks, it is certainly very difficult to make available that data to other people because it violates the kind of agreement between the lender and the borrower, ensuring that the information will not be made available to other entities. So that is the reason why I asked about the private and public compromise. But you said the private sector may play a more important role. Probably, but it is not market-orientated data that you can get for credit information. That is all the things about asymmetry and moral hazard which may include the difficulties and also secrecy of the data. Thank you.

Jongsoon Shin: Just two quick comments. So I fully understand the data privacy and that there is also a big trade-off on that. But the credit information also is a public good, so assuming that data privacy is maintained, I think it is a public good and, as in the chart I pointed out, there is a positive correlation between risk information sharing and loan availability. In order to have slightly smoother access to finance, the collection of the data will still matter. Thank you.

Suhaedi: Thank you, any other comments?

Salinee Wangtal: Yes, thank you. Just to add my thought to the earlier comment on the difficulties in getting credit information. I think the same can be said about the credit bureau for the other loans. Whether it is the consumer loans or the business loans, no borrowers would voluntarily offer their information. But it has to be done because it is a public good and it is good for the economy, it is good for the bank industry. More importantly, it should be good for the borrowers as well. It can be done and the way it is done is that you make it compulsory for borrowers to give consent to the lending agency, that there is an obligation for the lending agency to report both positive and negative information to the credit bureau.

This is how we did it in Thailand and I am sure that it is the practice in other countries as well. So this is the best way to ensure that we get plenty of this public good for the good of the nation and industry.

Suhaedi: Thank you for your insightful comments.

Jongsoon Shin: Just thank you very much for your thoughtful comments. I agree with that. So just to add one thing, the credit information is not only of benefit to lenders, but also to borrowers. It benefits the borrowers as well, because they can access their creditworthiness when they would like to have access to finance. So it also gives potential borrowers an incentive to meet their financial obligations and to review their creditworthiness. So this is a public good as well, as I mentioned. Thank you.

Suhaedi: Thank you, actually we have run out of time. One short question or comment from the floor, if any?

Naoyuki Yoshino: I have two very quick questions. Zombie firms as an ex-post, it is easy to tell those are zombie firms. But when you are looking forward and ahead whether the company will keep on growing or going down is very difficult to judge, especially in the case of bubbles. Many Japanese banks felt small and medium-sized real estate companies were growing, but after the burst of the bubble they became zombie firms. What is the best way to scrutinize zombie lending or not? Maybe the credit guarantee ratio should be differentiated bank by bank, based on the non-performing loan (NPL) ratio of each bank. So a differentiated credit guarantee ratio might avoid the lending to zombie firms. If any of you could answer, I am very glad to listen.

Participant: I think what I would like to add is that it seems we are quite concerned about lack of information, say the credit information of SMEs – small firms. But I think that the data is available, it is just about our willingness to dig up this data. I can tell you my one personal story. I asked my wife who used to work for a large commercial bank in Thailand. I said I am interested in these large Thai chemical companies. I want to know the borrowing of these companies, the internal finance and external finance. Not only that, I want to know if the borrowing and lending is through the supply chain, upstream and downstream, whether the banks have such information. She said yes and she can track the upstream and downstream on many levels, so for the borrowing and lending of these firms information is available, and not only that firm, but the firm that works with this particular firm has information as well.

So I asked her, can I have that information? She said no. So the data is there, the banks have got that type of information. So I can imagine that, if the monetary authorities would like to have that information, they can actually get that information. Whether they can make it publicly available or not, that is another question. Maybe they can protect the identity of the firms and make the data available for public use. I think that this is possible. So the information is available, it is just about whether we are willing to pick up this data. Because the data that we have been using so far is national-level data.

For example, in our work on these SMEs, about 8,000 firms, we used the World Bank data. This is possibly the best data so far if you want to look across the countries. The issue is that this data is survey data and the data that has questions like "Over the last fiscal year, please estimate the proportion of your working capital that was financed from internal funds, bank borrowing, and non-bank borrowing?" So if you ask for this information, you can imagine that there would be some overestimation or underestimation. So I think that this to some level has to do with the data collection.

As for the hard data, that cannot be obtained by survey. It has to come from the commercial banks and we cannot get that information from commercial banks, it has to be the monetary authorities. That again I think is a question of the willingness to dig up such data. So the data is there, but it is not available. That is my take on this.

Suhaedi: Thank you. As we have run out of time, I am sorry to all those who had wanted to ask questions and were not able to. In closing, please join me in thanking for excellent presenters and commentators. Thank you very much.

References

Beck T, Klapper LF, Mendoza JC (2008) The typology of partial credit guarantee funds around the world. The World Bank Policy Research Working Paper 4771. World Bank, Washington DC

Jinjarak Y, Mutuc PJ, Wignaraja G (2014) Does finance really matter for the participation of SMEs in international trade? Evidence from 8080 East Asian Firms. ADBI Working Paper No. 470. Asian Development Bank Institute, Tokyo. http://www.adbi.org/working-paper/2014/03/28/6218.finance.matter.smes.trade/ (Accessed 10 April 2014)

KPMG (2011) Credit access guarantees: a public asset between state and market. KPMG, Amstelveen, Netherlands

Lam WR, Shin J (2012) What role can financial policies play in revitalizing SMEs in Japan? IMF Working Paper 12/291

Mazzucato M (2013) The entrepreneurial state. Anthem, London

Organisation for Economic Co-operation and Development (2013) SME and entrepreneurship financing: the role of credit guarantee schemes and mutual guarantee societies in supporting finance for small and medium-sized enterprises. OECD, Amstelveen, Netherlands

Standard Chartered (2013) Asia leverage uncovered. Standard Chartered, London, UK

Tokuda H (2011) Searching for clues to the low profitability and competitiveness of Japanese SMEs: an analysis based upon international comparisons. Mizuho Research Paper No. 28 based on Mizuho Research Institute Ltd. (MHRI) and Bureau van Dijk, ORBIS

Session 3: Financial Inclusion and Financial Education

Tarisa Watanagase, Naoyuki Yoshino, Tomoyuki Furusawa, Peter Morgan, Victor Pontines, Ranee Jayamaha, Pungky P. Wibowo, and Julius Caesar Parreñas

Address by Session Chair

Tarisa Watanagase

Thank you. Good afternoon, ladies and gentlemen. Welcome back to the third session. First of all, let me thank the organizers—FSA, Japan, ADBI, and the IMF—for the kind invitation for me to take part in this very interesting and very timely conference, to chair the next session, and then to take part as a panelist in the following session.

This session will look at the issue of financial education. The lack of financial access in fact is a problem of the underprivileged or the disadvantaged segments of the economy. It could be an individual, it could be an SME, or a household. Usually, these segments are not underprivileged only in an economic sense, but also in

T. Watanagase
Bank of Thailand, Bangkok, Thailand

N. Yoshino
Financial Research Center (FSA Institute), Keio University, Tokyo, Japan

T. Furusawa
Policy and Legal Division, Planning and Coordination Bureau, Financial Services Agency, Tokyo, Japan

P. Morgan · V. Pontines
Asian Development Bank Institute, Tokyo, Japan

R. Jayamaha
Hatton National Bank PLC, Colombo, Sri Lanka

P. P. Wibowo
Financial Access and SME Development Department, Bank Indonesia, Jakarta, Indonesia

J. C. Parreñas
Bank of Tokyo-Mitsubishi UFJ, Ltd, Tokyo, Japan

ADB Institute, Financial Services Agency, Japan, International Monetary Fund Regional Office for Asia and the Pacific (eds.), *Financial System Stability, Regulation, and Financial Inclusion,* ADB Institute Series on Development Economics, DOI 10.1007/978-4-431-55254-3_5

other social aspects, including education, particularly with regards to the business and financial institutions.

Without basic knowledge of these issues they may not be able to get very far in improving their wellbeing and, likewise, it would be difficult for the authorities to try through that policy and policy implementation to increase the level of financial inclusion. The IFC's survey in 2010—I think someone in the earlier sessions mentioned this survey as well—showed that out of 400 million SMEs only 15 % have access to finance and 20 % have cited a lack of financial access as a major constraint on their businesses.

There are also 2.5 billion adults who lack access to a basic savings account. So getting financial education to these people in the underprivileged segments will definitely unleash the potential of these financially excluded people and will no doubt add substantially to economic growth and their wellbeing. So it will be a very interesting session.

We are very fortunate today to have quite a number of excellent resource persons, both from academia and practitioners, to share with us their experience and insights and perspectives on this very important issue.

Financial Education and Financial Inclusion[1]

Naoyuki Yoshino

Thank you very much for the introduction. I would like to spend about 10 min on the Japanese market figures of asset allocation and liabilities, and why financial education is needed in Japan. These are very appropriate figures of the US, Japan, and Germany (Fig. 1). The darkest part is share of deposits, the one next to it is the share of insurance and pensions, then securities, and the lightest gray part is stocks.

As you can see on the left-hand side, the US is very well balanced. In Japan, it is dominated by deposits and life insurance. Germany is in between Japan and the US. The US was very quick to recover from the financial crisis because the housing loan problem, as you can see from the red part in the US, the deposit share, is very small. And furthermore, the nonperforming loans of those assets have been securitized so, in the US case, banks did not keep nonperforming loans for so long. But in the Japanese case, the share of deposits is very large and they have kept on holding their nonperforming loans for so long that it delays the recovery of the Japanese economy.

This figure is the share of deposits at the bottom, and life insurance is the second from the bottom, and you can see more than 70 % of assets are allocated to deposits and life insurance (Fig. 2). Life insurance in Japan is regarded as long-term savings. The Japanese people prefer very safe assets and also short-term and long-term asset management.

This is the age profile of who owns financial assets in Japan (Table 1). As you can see, the bottom is over 70 years of age. They are the richest people in Japan.

[1] The views expressed in this presentation are those of the author and do not necessarily reflect the views of the Financial Services Agency or the FSA Institute.

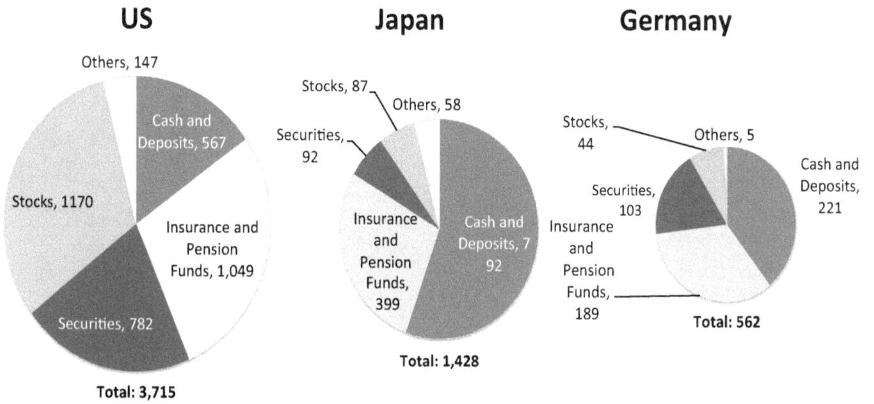

Fig. 1 Households' asset allocation. (Source: Yoshino and Kaji 2013)

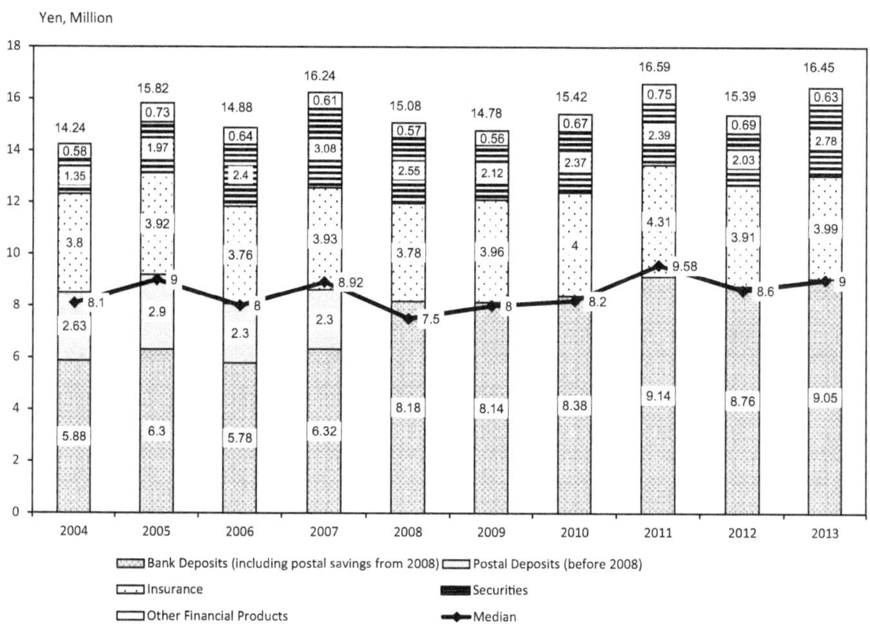

Fig. 2 Allocation of households' financial assets. (Source: Bank of Japan flow of funds data (yearly) https://www.boj.or.jp/en/statistics/sj/index.htm/)

Then, 60 years of age is the second lowest. They tend to make just deposits and they have not so much of a financial education. As you can see here, the top figure is the aging population where the number of aged people will be increasing. So I think how to allocate those aged assets into various sectors will also be important in financial education.

The next page is the survey of for what kind of reasons people select financial institutions (Fig. 3). You can see from the third line from the bottom, principal guar-

Table 1 Financial assets by age. (Source: Bank of Japan 2013b)

	Deposits	Insurance	Securities	Others	Total
Average	635	303	179	52	1,169
20 years	*266*	26	40	10	342
30 years	298	122	77	40	537
40 years	355	241	85	62	743
50 years	533	344	126	65	1,068
60 years	811	409	*276*	43	1,539
70 years	*1,035*	333	*287*	52	1,707

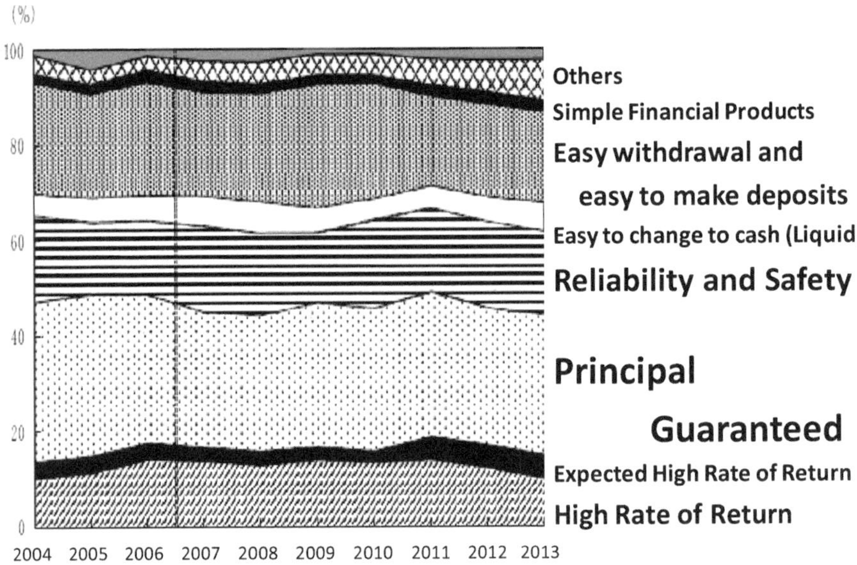

Fig. 3 Reasons to select financial institution. (Source: Bank of Japan 2013a)

antee is the largest, then reliability and safety, and the third largest reason is easy withdrawal and easy to make deposits. So those are the major reasons why Japanese people prefer to put their money in them. Of course we prefer safety, but our rate of return—you can see in this figure in dividends and interest receipts divided by income—is the lowest among all major countries, because we very much tend toward safety and security (Fig. 4).

Another reason why our rate of return is very low will be the fees and commissions of the distributor system. Household investors are maximizing their rate of return. However, distributors receive commissions and trust fees from asset management companies and the investors, so their objective function is different from investors. I think in order to make our asset management much more efficient, the distributor fees and commission mechanism have to be changed.

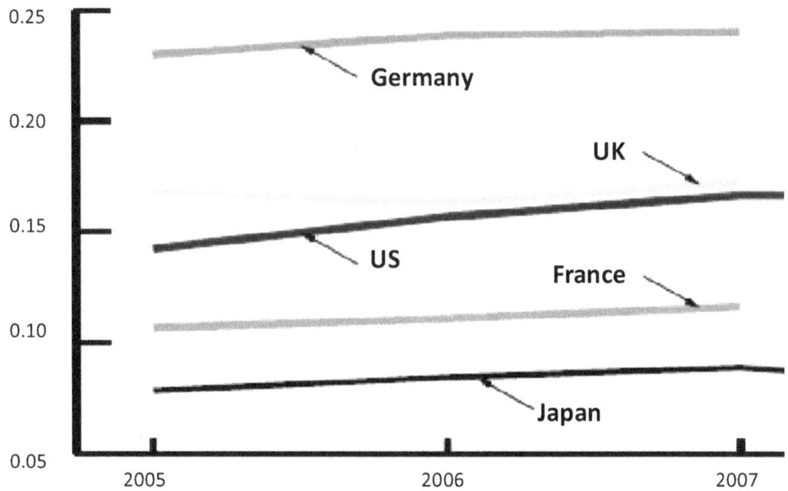

Fig. 4 Dividends and interest receipt/Income. (Source: Yoshino and Kaji 2013)

Currently, number two, is principal plus dividend times some amount of ratio is the trust fees and commissions. But we should change it to just dividends and rate of return times alpha excluding principal, which will make the distributors and investors have the same objective function. So institutional changes will also be needed in order to increase the Japanese households' asset management.

We have long-term financial assets like pension funds and investments, but as you can see in the second line, many investors in pension funds rotate every 2–3 years. So their incentive mechanism is very different from a long-term-oriented one. Furthermore, number two, we do not have 401 K type pension funds and we have defined benefits rather than contributors decision of self-responsibility, i.e., defined contribution. Then, the last line shows investors prefer just safe assets and invest in government bonds. So we have to also change the institutional mechanisms. Also, the compensation and bonus systems of Japan are very conservative, which is very different from the US.

In this case, the bonuses and salaries are based on performance. But in the Japanese case, they are not so much related to performance, so people prefer to have safer assets rather than seek greater return. Probably, the bonuses and salary system may have to be changed a little.

The financial education of Japan. When I was very small, many Japanese thought we should work hard and make deposits. But it is not so honest to earn money through financial investment. That was the basic feature of the Japanese way of thinking, so that is why our rate of return here is the lowest among all major Organisation for Economic Co-operation and Development (OECD) countries. Financial education is very important in secondary schools, high schools, but not in the second line. Most of the teachers in financial education are in geography and history. Financial education is taught in geography and history sections.

Primary school teachers are teaching financial education in their home-making courses. Unfortunately, there are not so many professionals in primary and second-

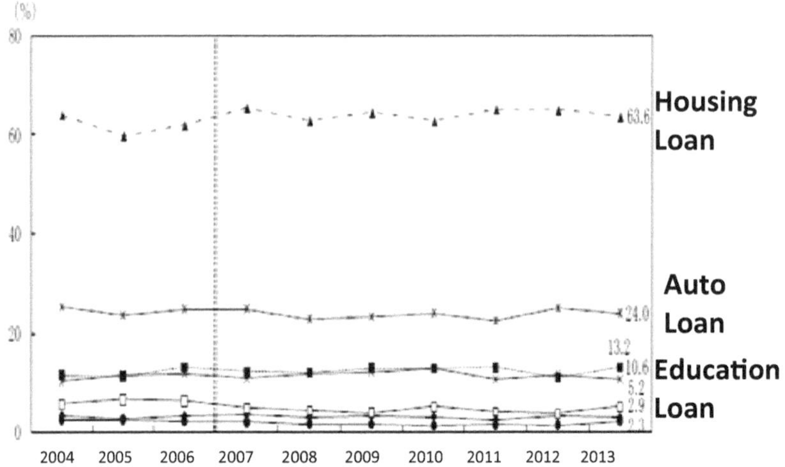

Fig. 5 Households' borrowings in Japan. (Source: Bank of Japan 2013a)

ary schools to teach that financial education. We probably need some educational changes to teach children how to make their savings in an efficient manner.

The next topic is the liability side. Financial education is important not only for asset management, but also for the borrowing side (Fig. 5). Japan has the highest debt in housing loans—60 % of household debt is housing loans. The second largest is 24 %, for automobile loans, followed by education loans, and so on. For housing loans, the present discounted value of how to compute their interest rate and so on are also very important and it is also related to auto loans. Japan had very huge household default around 2003–2004. The year 1990 saw the burst of the bubble. After the burst of the bubble, our household debt started to increase and the number of household defaults has since increased very drastically.

Many Asian countries are faced with loan sharks and household defaults are increasing very rapidly. Japan introduced a new law to regulate microfinance and microcredit regulations. First, the total amount of borrowing has to be lower than one-third of income, and second, the highest rate of interest rate was set at up to 20 %. Then, borrower information was aggregated and paper examination was introduced to money lenders. These efforts have contributed to the reduction of household defaults and to making loan sharks leave the market. For a better way to reduce loan sharks and so on, institutional regulations will also be needed.

The last two topics are how to utilize all the people's money in risk-related sectors (Fig. 6). Banking account, the darker shaded part, is mainly invested into safer borrowers because of lots of regulation, but we have a lack of venture capital in Japan and many Asian countries. I was proposing hometown investment trust funds. This is a regional trust fund that is invested into regional projects, such as wind power and solar power and small businesses in the agriculture sector. These loans are face-to-face and one-to-one, so each person knows where it is invested. Of course, the principal is not guaranteed, but it is invested into community projects and agricultural farmers, and many people know where it is invested. I hope this

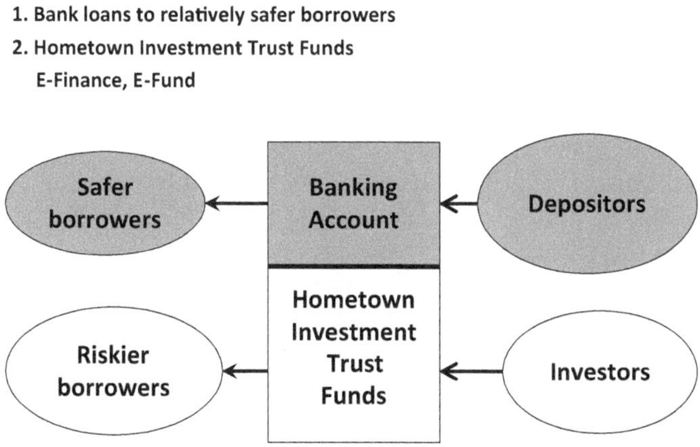

Fig. 6 Bank-based small and medium-sized enterprise financing and regional financing to riskier borrowers. (Source: Yoshino 2012)

kind of hometown investment trust funds could be growing in those regions where many old people want to help the region. This kind of mechanism will be implemented, hopefully, in other Asian regions.

The last topic is SME lending. In the previous session, there was a discussion about SMEs. In Japan, SMEs also require lots of education. An SME database was started about 10 years ago. The credit risk database (CRD) at the bottom was created about 13 years ago and they have started to collect data. In order to create a database, SME owners have to keep books and also have to report to those databases. That has become a very good education for SMEs. SMEs have no bookkeeping and they are just doing their business based on their daily conditions. But the collection of data for the database on SMEs will help to educate them on how to collect data. To get a better picture of what is going on in their business could make the SME president and households much more inclined to add to the database, and make them think about their businesses much more.

So I think teaching SMEs how to gather data for their business database will help to enhance the education method. Because of time constraints, I would like to stop here. Thank you very much.

Developments of Financial Education in Japan[2]

Tomoyuki Furusawa

Thank you very much. Because Professor Yoshino covered all the topics concerning Japanese education, I just want to talk a little about the overall strategy of Japanese education, which complements what was said earlier on the topic financial education.

[2] The views expressed in this presentation are those of the author and do not necessarily reflect the views of the Financial Services Agency or the FSA Institute.

First, I would like to cover a little the global situation concerning financial education. Since the financial crisis, as you may be well aware, a growing number of governments have engaged in the development of dedicated national study strategies on financial education. It is often said that such strategies should have three pillars. The first one is the enhancement of financial literacy, and it is quite clear. The second one is broadening the spectrum of financial inclusion, especially through the growing numbers of middle class families. The third pillar might be the upgrading of the level of financial consumer protection.

I think there are two backgrounds concerning this development. The first one perhaps mainly concerns the success in the economic management of many developing countries, especially including the Southeast Asian countries. As a result of that success, we observe the rapid expansion of the middle class in those countries. The governments of those countries in particular are aware of the need for financial literacy and financial inclusion to accommodate the needs of those newly created middle classes.

The efforts of those governments will produce the foundation for more robust economic growth. This has a virtuous cycle effect. It means that the growth of the middle class and the enhancement of financial literacy may contribute to the next step of financial growth in the overall economy. That is one background of the enhancement of financial education in recent years.

As for the developed countries, the situation is a bit different. The financial crisis itself has a galvanizing impact on those countries, especially the so-called subprime loan products have a very important impact on those economies. In those countries, financial consumers are surrounded by very, very sophisticated or sometimes too complicated financial products. As Professor Yoshino showed, the fee structure is a bit opaque and the risk profile and fee structures are sometimes very difficult to understand for retail investors.

At the same time, because of national budget constraints, public and occupational welfare benefits for middle-class people are shrinking, so middle-class families have to prepare for retirement on their own. Of course, Japan is not an exception in this trend and the Japanese FSA is trying very hard to be the leader in this development, especially by closely cooperating with the Bank of Japan.

This is the overall structure of the players concerning financial education in Japan. As you can see, the FSA has three missions and the second mission is protecting not only depositors but also financial investors or financial service consumers. So the protection of those people is one of the main missions of the FSA. Up to now, the target of financial education has been mainly focused on households, as you can see. Because, as I have said, there is an asymmetry of financial knowledge between financial intermediaries and households, we have to amend that asymmetry through financial education. At the same time, we have recently been paying more attention to the financial education of enterprises, including SMEs, and bookkeeping in particular is one of the main topics concerning the financial education of SMEs.

I want to show a bit of the history of financial education in Japan. Actually, we started this effort at the beginning of this century, which means the year 2000. We revised the deposit protection system that year and the Japanese FSA emphasized the importance of the financial education program in 2000. Subsequently, the first national strategy was introduced in 2005. It sets the agenda for financial and economic education. As you can see at the bottom, it was updated in April last year in the report of the study group on financial education.

As you can see, there were very important developments at the global level in 2012, with the G20 leaders' Los Cabos Summit declaration, in which the high-level principle of national strategies for financial education was endorsed and shared by those leaders. The FSA report or revision of the national strategy is in line with that development as well. It says that one of the key persons or key players of financial education in Japan is the so-called Center Council for Financial Services Information (CCFSI), which also has a local division and is a local council for financial services. Those are the key strategies of financial education in Japan. They are based on the classical cooperation between the Bank of Japan and the Japanese FSA.

The key major tasks of those efforts are to be focused on the following three pillars. The first one is to define what is to be learned at what age group; the second is to promote the interlinkage of the websites of the relevant organizations including deposit takers, insurers, and broker dealers; and the third pillar is to include the function of the diagnosis of life learning on the CCFSI's website. We are currently putting quite a lot of resources into developing a so-called map to define what we learn at what age.

The key image is as follows. We have to give different factors, different guidelines and different materials to each target group. We need a special program for elementary students. We need special guidance for junior high school students. We have a particular course for university students and we often have a very similar program for senior people. They are very vulnerable to the asymmetry of financial information, so we have to create special programs for those different target groups.

This is the report summary and currently we are developing this sort of map. Perhaps this year is a very important year to strengthen our efforts to spread this information to retail investors. Thank you very much.

Financial Stability and Financial Inclusion

Peter Morgan

Good afternoon, ladies and gentlemen. The title of our presentation is Financial Stability and Financial Inclusion. The reason for this is that it is widely believed that both financial stability and financial inclusion are important, but the relationship between the two is not so clear. Are they complementary, or are there trade-offs between them? There is actually surprisingly little research done on this topic. First I will talk about the relation between financial stability and financial inclusion data and issues, the stylized facts, and some previous work in this area. Then my co-author Victor Pontines will talk about our modeling approach and the conclusions.

In terms of the relationship between the two, I will talk a little about the definitions and dimensions of financial stability, the same for financial inclusion, and then talk a bit about the channels for interaction between them.

As for a definition of financial stability, this is the hard part. There have been many attempts, it is not easy to define. Perhaps it is easier to recognize financial instability, but one example is that financial stability "…can be defined as a condition in which the financial system comprising of financial intermediaries, markets, and market infrastructure is capable of withstanding shocks and the unraveling of financial balances, thereby mitigating the likelihood of disruptions in the financial intermediation process, which are severe enough to significantly impair the allocation of savings to profitable investment opportunities" (ECB 2012) So this resilience to disruption is quite an important aspect of financial stability.

We can divide aspects into two main parts according to the literature, one is pro-cyclicality, which is mechanisms that operate within the financial system and between it and the macro economy and can generate outside financial cycles and business fluctuations. Then the other is interconnectedness, which is common exposures and interlinkages in the financial system that result in joint failures of financial institutions by making them vulnerable to common sources of risk.

If we look at some of the sources of these two financial system risks, for procyclicality there are the well-known feedback loops between bank capital and lending, asset value and bank lending, exchange rate exposure, and balance sheet interactions. The one I would like to focus on here is the liquidity aspect, because to the extent that banks are dependent on what is called non-core financing, that is, financing outside bank deposits, that does introduce a source of risk because of the imbalance of maturity between assets and liabilities. As you will see, this is one way that the financial inclusion aspect can come in.

On the interconnectedness side, common exposures to similar asset classes are a very important feature of this and we will see that if you have financial inclusion that can actually give you greater diversity in terms of the financial assets of banks and thereby reduce risk that way.

Now the definition of financial inclusion is fairly straightforward, so let me skip ahead. In terms of what are expected interactions between financial inclusion and financial stability, on the positive side is financial sector diversification. That is, larger and more diverse bank assets can contribute to the resiliency of the banks' balance sheet on the asset side. On the liability side, the small savers can contribute to deposit base size and stability and therefore reduce the dependence on non-core financing. Secondly, there can be better transmission of monetary policy throughout the economy and, third, there could also be improved surveillance of money laundering.

On the negative side, promotion of inclusion could lower asset quality. Obviously, the subprime lending story is a classic example of that. Outsourcing by banks could increase reputational risk and there could be new risks from specialized microfinance institutions.

Going on to data source and issues, there are basically two relevant datasets. One is the World Bank Global Financial Development database, which has 164 countries and 61 years, although there are a lot of blank spots in those years as we will find out. Then there is the IMF Financial Access Survey, which includes 193 countries and has about 11 years of data. Now the good news is that data on financial stability

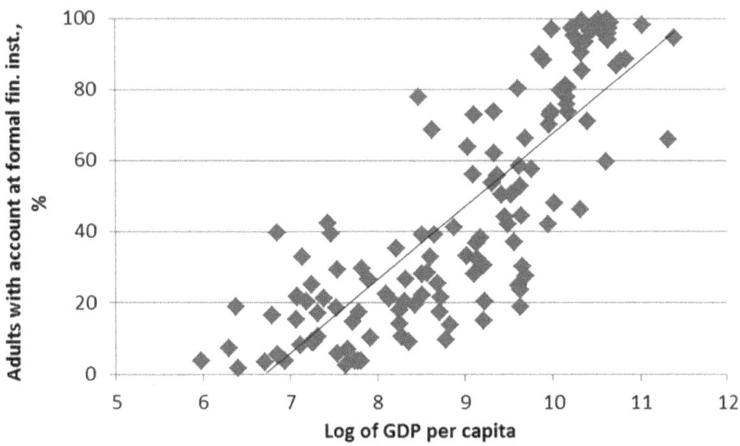

Fig. 7 Stylized facts—share of adults with accounts at formal institutions strongly related to income. *GDP* gross domestic product. (Source: World Bank 2012)

are relatively available, but the problem is that the data on financial inclusion are quite sparse.

On some items we have up to 10 years of data: things like number of bank branches in a country, but only one or two years of data on small firm access and only one year, which is 2011, on household access to bank deposits and loans. So it is basically a cross-section, not a time series. Even within those very limited time frames we have lots of missing data, so, unfortunately, sparse data is a problem in this area.

In terms of the kinds of variables that we are looking at, for measures of financial stability we look at the percentage of nonperforming loans, banks' Z-score which is a measure of bank quality, deposit volatility over the cycle, again looking at the funding issue and also we have data on banking crises from sources like Rogoff and Reinhart. Then financial inclusion measures include many things like the number of bank branches, bank accounts, ATMs per thousand persons; firms with deposits or line of credit, percent of total SMEs with deposits or line of credit; adults with deposit at formal, financial institutions and adults borrowing or saving in the past year, both as a percent of the total.

Now just to look at some of the stylized facts. The first point is that inclusion is pretty well correlated with income (Fig. 7). This chart shows the log of GDP per capita versus the percentage of adults with accounts at formal financial institutions. You can see there is a nice positive relationship. On the other hand, there is a fair amount of diversity. Obviously, there are other things going on there too.

Secondly, however, there is rather little correlation of adults with access at formal national institutions to bank NPLs (Fig. 8). You can see basically a flat line, so we are not doing very well there. And secondly, if you look at banks' Z-scores, also again not much correlation with the share of adults with formal bank accounts. So that particular route is so far not very productive. We are doing a bit better when

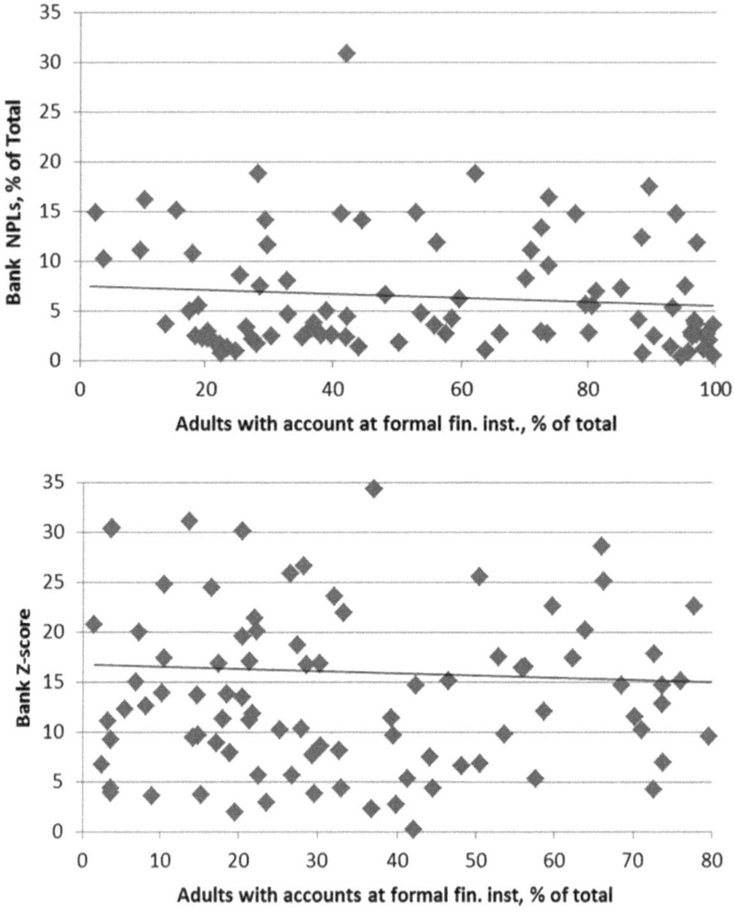

Fig. 8 Stylized facts—little correlation of adult account access with financial stability. *NPL* non-performing loan. (Source: World Bank 2012)

you look at the SME share of outstanding loans as a percent of total. That does seem to have some negative correlation with bank nonperforming loans, which is the relationship that you would expect (Fig. 9). So that is a bit promising. On the other hand, if you look at the banks' Z-score you get the wrong sign in terms of the slope (Fig. 10). It is still very early days in this data analysis and the data shortage is also a bit of a problem.

Now I will just talk a little about the previous empirical work, a couple of studies we can cite. First, Adasme, Majnoni, and Uribe (Adasme et al. 2006) found that NPLs of small firms have quasi- normal loss distributions, while those of large firms have fat tail distributions. So the systemic risk of the former is less, so that again banks can diversify their risk by having more SMEs loans. Then, Han and Melecky (2013) looked at the volatility of bank deposits during crisis periods and

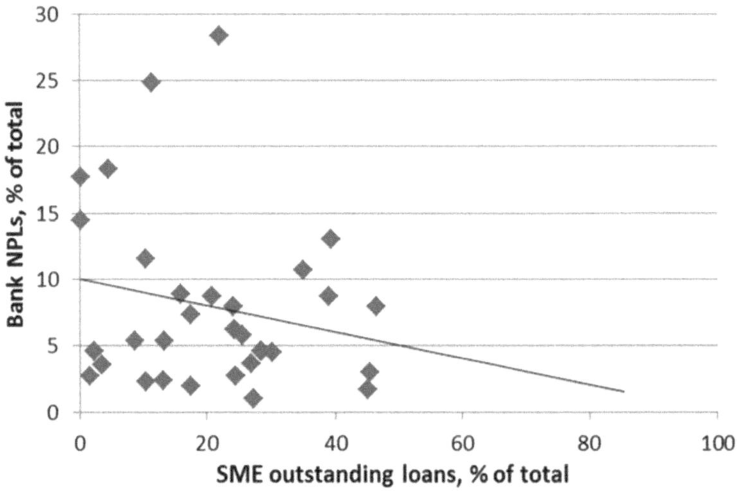

Fig. 9 Stylized facts—some correlation of SME lending share with bank NPLs. *NPL* nonperforming loan, *SMEs* small and medium-sized enterprises. (Source: IMF 2013)

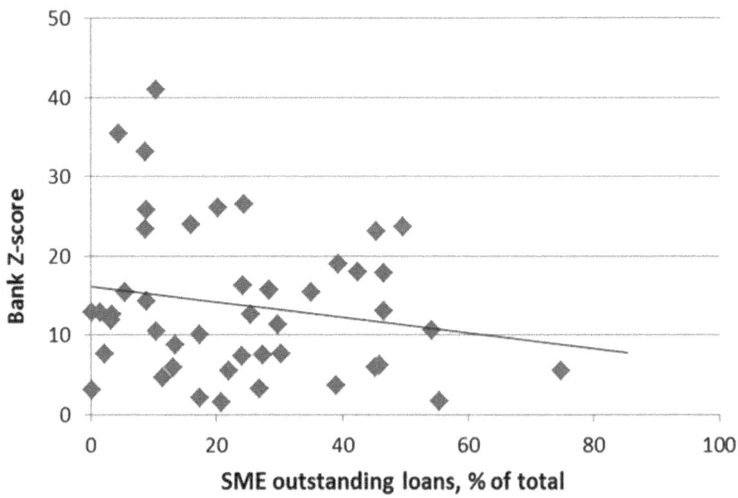

Fig. 10 Stylized facts—but correlation of SME lending share with bank Z-score has wrong sign. *SMEs* small and medium-sized enterprises. (Source: IMF 2013)

they found that a greater share of people with bank deposits tends to reduce the volatility of total bank deposits during economic downturns. That specifically a 10 % increase of the share of people that have access to bank deposits can reduce the deposit growth drops or deposit withdrawal rates by about 3–8 percentage points. That is quite an interesting result.

I will now transfer to Victor who will tell us about our work. Thank you.

- To formally verify the link between financial access and financial stability, the regression model below was used:

$$finstab_i = \alpha(finaccess_i) + \beta X_i + \varepsilon_i$$

- $finstab_i$ uses cross-country (i) data on Bank Z-score (bzs_i) and Bank NPLs (npl_i) and both measures are transformed as follows:
  $finstab_i$ (1) = minimum value between 2007–2011 – average value between 2001–2006
  $finstab_i$ (2) = minimum value between 2007–2011 – maximum value between 2001–2006
- $finaccess_i$: includes cross-country data on:
  - Firms with Line of Credit to Total Firms (%) (fc_i),
  - Small Firms with Line of Credit to Total Small Firms (sfc_i) (%), and
  - SME Outstanding Loans to Outstanding Loans of Commercial Banks (%) ($smel_i$)
- Vector of control variables (X_i) includes:
  - constant term
  - GDP per capita ($lggdp_i$),
  - Private credit by deposit money banks and other financial institutions to GDP (%) ($cgdp_i$),
  - Liquid assets to deposits and short-term funding (%) (liq_i),
  - Non-FDI capital flow to GDP (%) ($nfdi_i$), and
  - Financial Openness ($opns_i$)
- Average data for 2001–2006 financial access measures and control variables used to control forendogeneity

Fig. 11 Our approach—model. (Source: Authors)

Financial Stability and Financial Inclusion (contd)

Victor Pontines

Good afternoon. My part today is to quickly complete the remainder of our presentation. To formally verify the link between financial access and financial stability, we actually used this cross-country regression model as presented there in Fig. 11. So we have financial stability as our left-hand side variable and then some measures of financial access as of the independent variables on the right-hand side and some control variables, which are referred to as X. So we used two measures of financial stability: one is the bank Z-score, which Peter mentioned, and then also the commercial banks' nonperforming loans as a proportion of total bank loans.

Both of these measures were actually transformed as follows. For the first one we actually take the difference between the minimum value between 2007 and 2011 with the average value of these two measures between 2001 and 2006. Then for the second transform measure we take the difference between the minimum value of these two measures between 2007 and 2011 and the maximum value of these two financial stability measures between 2001 and 2006.

Among the many numbers of financial access measures that were mentioned by Peter, we actually used three specific measures of financial access. The first one is the line of credit to total firms, which were referred to in the estimation as *fc*. Second is the small firms with line of credit to total small firms which were referred to in the later estimation as *sfc*. And the third one is the SMEs' outstanding loans to total outstanding loans of commercial banks, which is referred to as *smel*. We also have a vector of control variables, X_i. Then we take the average data of all these measures of financial access and our control variables *X* for 2001 and 2006 in order to control for endogeneity in our estimation.

Table 2 Estimation results 1. (Source: Authors' estimates)

	bzs(1)	bzs(2)
Fc	0.286**	
	(0.109)	
sfc		0.299**
		(0.132)
lggdp	−0.343	−0.324
	(1.138)	(1.219)
cgdp	−0.235**	−0.234**
	(0.097)	(0.116)
liq	0.079	0.071
	(0.063)	(0.070)
nfdi	0.045	0.066
	(0.061)	(0.063)
opns	0.030	0.036
	(0.025)	(0.030)
R^2	0.556	0.469
n	23	23

Values in parentheses are robust-standard errors
** = significant at 5% level, *** = significant at 1% level

In this case, in these estimated results for the bank Z-score, the first row of Table 2 gives you the first measure of financial access, i.e., the share of small firm borrowers to total firm borrowers, and the relationship is positive. Then *sfc* in the second row, which is the share of lending of small firms to total lending of small firms, is also positively related to the bank Z-score (Table 2). To be sure, our estimation is quite simple in that we are not going to make any strong claims with our result, given the fact that our results are very much preliminary because of the very small sample size, the problems of which were raised by Peter.

Then we have here our representation of results for our second financial stability measure, which is nonperforming loans as a proportion of total commercial bank loans. You can see here that *fc* is found to be negative while *sfc* is also found to be negative, which means that if financial access measures increase, NPLs will actually go down (Table 3).

To conclude our presentation, financial inclusion could have both positive and negative implications for financial stability. Positive in the sense that diversification of bank assets and increased stability of deposit base improves stability; and negative because you could have erosion of credit standards, et cetera, as suggested by the subprime loan experience in the US. Financial inclusion data is problematic because of the short time span and the sparseness of the database.

We also find some evidence that an increased share of lending to SMEs aided financial stability mainly through reduction of NPLs and the probability of default by financial institutions. Thank you very much.

Table 3 Estimation results 2. (Source: Authors' estimates)

	NPL(1)	NPL(2)
fc	−0.173** (0.082)	
sfc		−0.136* (0.082)
lggdp	−2.285 (3.750)	−2.955 (4.116)
cgdp	0.208** (0.091)	0.222** (0.098)
liq	−0.051 (0.128)	−0.251 (0.138)
nfdi	−0.448** (0.223)	−0.490* (0.249)
opns	−0.044** (0.019)	−0.051** (0.021)
R^2	0.513	0.462
n	16	16

Values in parentheses are robust-standard errors
* = significant at 10% level, ** = significant at 5% level.

Comments to Session 3

Ranee Jayamaha

Thank you very much for the opportunity given to comment on the presentations. I was delighted to listen to three very interesting presentations and the research outcomes contained therein. It will also be interesting to compare the applicability of the research results to different country situations.

Professor Yoshino's paper refers to the more conscious attitude of Japanese communities regarding the safety of their savings, rather than seeking higher returns. It is in sharp contrast to the situation in many South Asian countries, where people appear to be chasing after higher interest rates for numerous reasons and often resent being cheated by fraudulent companies which offer higher rates than formal financial institutions. Japanese savers are unique in that they are more concerned about the safety of their funds.

One of the main reasons for the neglect of safety by savers seems to be the lack of financial education and literacy in addition to greed. Way back in the 1980s and the 1990s, most of the Asian countries experienced the failure of a number of financial institutions that were subsequently restructured through consolidation, mergers, and acquisitions. For example, Singapore and Malaysia have already completed the process, while India and Sri Lanka are still undergoing the consolidation process.

It is also important to note that the central banks in South Asia play a key role in enhancing financial education and literacy in their respective countries. Many central banks and governments have introduced new laws and regulations while amending the existing ones to ensure that supervisors and regulators have the necessary powers for effective supervision.

It is also interesting to note that a significant proportion of the loans by banking institutions in Japan account for housing loans. The proportions may differ in the rest of Asia. Generally, commercial banks are reluctant to accommodate housing loans largely due to recovery issues, but the situation seems to be different in Japan. It appears that credit discipline and culture are well entrenched in Japanese society compared with other Asia countries.

Having learnt the bitter results from the Asian crisis, banks and financial institutions (BFIs) are reluctant to increase their exposure to real estate development in many of the Asian countries. Central banks dissuade commercial banks from having high exposure to real estate development and therefore the contribution of banks to housing bubbles is not very significant.

The paper also referred to SME lending, which is a very significant factor in many Asian countries. Governments have taken numerous steps to promote the SME sector. BFIs have realized the importance of SMEs in sustainable development and have taken a number of measures to increase lending for SME activities.

Mr. Furusawa's paper refers to financial education and financial inclusion, both of which are significant and important for sustainable development. The paper reveals the well-structured and tiered financial education and inclusion programs in Japan and their wide spread across all segments of society. In Japan, the financial education process starts at the school level and moves on to the secondary and tertiary (university) level. Japan appears to be well ahead of other countries in adult education. The well-structured and widely spread Japanese financial education program should be admired for its continuity and effectiveness.

Although countries like India, Sri Lanka, and Malaysia have started financial education and inclusion programs, a lot more work is required to roll out such programs to all segments of their populations covering the entire countries. BFIs in Sri Lanka conduct island wide school savers' programs and such programs not only help further financial education but also enable BFIs to collect low-cost funding. Often, BFIs also assist schools in numerous educational programs to enhance financial education among students, while the universities have amended their curricula to include financial education and literacy as important subject areas.

Reference has been made to the deposit guarantee schemes. If these deposit guarantee schemes are likely to prolong the existence of weak financial institutions, it is tantamount to weak institutions being subsidized by stronger ones. That is the moral hazard side of deposit insurance schemes, although funds in such schemes can be used to pay depositors. In addition, deposit guarantee schemes give the public confidence to stay in the formal financial system. For example, Federal Deposit Insurance in the US has been providing assistance on numerous occasions to the banks that experienced difficulties as a result of the subprime crisis and other financial disruptions. Another example is Sri Lanka, which has a deposit insurance fund and also provides distress loan facilities to troubled institutions.

The attempts by almost all countries in Asia to use information and communication technology (ICT) for financial inclusion are commendable. Many of the ICT developments have been integrated into financial education and financial inclusion in South Asia. BFIs in most countries are heavily dependent on ICT to provide convenient and safe banking and financial services to their clients. For example, mobile phones are used as an effective and convenient instrument for value transfers. Such value transfers can be large volumes with low values or they can be low values with large volumes. Asia is going through an ICT revolution that helps multi-channel banking and financial services. Bangladesh, Sri Lanka, and parts of India, use ICT to make financial instruments more effective for developing inclusion and education.

People do not have to be taught or coached to use mobile phones. Newer instruments and facilities provided through innovation in ICT help to further financial education and financial inclusion. The whole of Asia as well as South Asia has benefited from innovation. For example, in Sri Lanka knowledge centers (approximately 800) covering all provinces help adult education in the country. These centers conduct programs to enhance ICT knowledge and financial education.

The third paper by Morgan and Pontines presents an excellent attempt to establish the correlation between financial stability and financial inclusion. The fundamental question is whether financial inclusion leads to financial instability? From a hind sight the answer is not necessarily. The extension of banking and financial services to the grass root level can be advantageous to many people. Perhaps multi-channel payments and delivery systems could be added as proxies to represent financial inclusion and they may yield some interesting results. This is because the narrow definition of financial inclusion and bank branch based models are no longer relevant compared with the situation that prevailed many years ago. The payment system is a pillar of financial stability and it can be used as a proxy for financial stability. If a payment system is unaffordable, inflexible, and complex, it cannot be accessed by the general public. That is financial exclusion. Financial inclusion can be enhanced through multi-channel banking products and services as well.

From the research outcomes of these analyses we can derive three very important policy prescriptions. Firstly, financial education and financial inclusion should be declared a national policy. They should be treated as public goods. When they are part of national policy, policymakers, practitioners, and BFIs will take the necessary measures to promote them.

Secondly, it would be relevant to capture financial inclusion through the usage of multi-channel financial access and multi-channel financial delivery. This applies to the retail, SME, and microfinance sectors. In this regard, newer financial instruments and innovative products can be used as proxies to capture the impact.

Thirdly, as access to finance by the underprivileged communities in South East Asia is still a problem, it may be useful to conduct an impact assessment of the measures initiated by the relevant authorities to enhance financial inclusion.

Those are my comments. Thank you very much.

Pungky P. Wibowo

Distinguished speakers, colleagues, ladies and gentlemen, good afternoon. Firstly I would like to say thank you to ADBI, the IMF, and the Japanese FSA for having such a very important and prestigious discussion about financial education, financial stability, and financial inclusion.

First of all, before I tell you what has been the Indonesian experience with conducting financial education, let me start with a few words focusing on financial education and financial inclusion, a topic firstly presented by Professor Naoyuki Yoshino from the FSA Institute and Keio University. Aligned with Professor Yoshino's presentation, Indonesia also has the view that the household sector not only has an important role in the economy, but also has a great influence on the financial stability system. The influence of the household sector on the financial system can be seen from the amount of bank loans to households. But often incorrect management and liquidity of households could potentially lead to failure of households in meeting their debt obligations.

Then the regular and intensive survey and analysis of the development of households' financial conditions becomes a very important and strategic activity to be conducted by the financial authorities. The survey will be of benefit to the financial authorities, such as central banks. It will be useful not only for formulation of strategies for crisis prevention, but also to help formulate policies to boost household economic activity in the country, including raising the level of financial household inclusion. In addition, the analysis of the financial condition of households will support the financial authorities in their efforts to maintain the stability of the financial system with a view to long-term sustainable development.

Bank Indonesia has been conducting annual household balance surveys since 2007. The purpose of these surveys is to determine how many households have access to finance and to maintain surveillance of the household financial sector. The results of the survey show the proportions of household savings held by banks, nonbanks, and non-financial institutions, and it reveals the proportion of un-banked households. Based on these findings, Bank Indonesia, along with the government, mapped out its strategy to enhance financial inclusion. We believe the resilience of the financial sector is not only influenced by macroeconomic conditions, but also by household factors such as consumption, savings, and household balances. The household survey 2011 found that of all respondents only 48 % had a savings account with formal financial institutions. 45 % of respondents had credit. Of those who had credit, 90 % got their credit from banks, 16 % from non-bank financial institutions, and 24 % from non-financial institutions. Those who engaged with formal financial institutions can be a potential customer for the bank and non-bank financial institutions. This is part of the financial inclusion program.

In the real sector, to overcome the lack of financial record data, Bank Indonesia has started an SME rating pilot project in 2012. The methodology for conducting the survey covered management risk, business risk, and financial risk. The objectives of the pilot project are to assess the willingness of SMEs to be surveyed in order to obtain the ratings, and also to assess the effectiveness of the rating results in the loan approval process.

The long-term proposal for the SME rating program is to be aligned with the national agenda for the regional credit guarantee system and increased access of SMEs to financial services.

With interest, we listened to the presentation about the development of financial education in Japan, presented by Mr. Tomoyuki Furusawa from the Japanese Financial Services Agency. I have a few comments. First, the central bank needs to make financial education a priority, to increase the effectiveness of central bank policy and as part of its social responsibility. The better people understand finance and the economy, the better central bank policy transmission will be.

Financial education requires a strong commitment from related parties, which are represented in the national strategy on financial education. In this regard, we are very proud of the recent launch of the financial education strategy by the Indonesian Financial Services Authority, which aims to increase the effectiveness of financial education. It needs coordination and collaboration among institutions. This cooperation framework can be implemented through national coordination, from responses of related ministers and other stakeholders. A financial survey has an important role in creating a financial education strategy. The survey is the baseline for mapping the country's financial situation through collecting information on many aspects that should be focused on in terms of increasing the financial literacy level, such as identifying a number of target groups, composing a financial education strategy, and setting program indicators.

Personally, I support Japan's strategy, which is a well-thought-out plan, setting targets for financial education. Setting specific targets will determine education materials, the scope of financial education materials, and means a bigger chance of getting optimal results. Getting involved in the international forums and gaining experience from them gives a useful advantage for the members to listen to each other on their experiences with financial inclusion, particularly on financial education. For instance, the high-level principle of a national strategy for financial education endorsed by G20 leaders in 2013 can easily be adopted by members by making some adjustments to social demography, culture, local wisdom, and preferences in their country. Lastly, review of monitoring and evaluation has also played an important part in ensuring financial education programs attain the targets that have been set and lead to optimum results.

Ladies and gentlemen, the presentation by Peter Morgan and Victor Pontines of ADBI about financial stability and financial inclusion showed us the value of information. I would like to make some comments on it.

First, financial inclusion has implications for financial stability. Based on their presentation, the impact would be positive or negative. In order to have a bigger chance of achieving a positive impact, I believe that innovation in financial inclusion should involve more ways to draw attention to the importance of financial education. It is also because in talking about financial inclusion, it means we also acknowledge the importance of having the right strategy for all financial education.

Through financial education, we build awareness in society and try to achieve the goal of a change in financial behavior. To reach this goal, we believe financial education should start at an early age. A different approach should be adopted for different target groups when communicating financial education. The education should include basic financial planning, banking products and services, and complaint and dispute resolution.

Based on the presentation by Morgan and Pontines on page 11, about financial stability and financial inclusion variables, we would like to highlight several things.

We hope to see soon some results about the extent of financial regulation on financial inclusion to be considered as one of the variables in your equation, so we could have the better prediction whether the financial stability could be also supported by financial inclusion activities, including the supporting regulation. This evidence supports the common understanding that a well-functioning and inclusive financial system could help mitigate the effects of information asymmetries and reduce transaction costs. The classic process of market failure followed by boosting of economic growth, spreading equality of opportunities, promoting redistribution of wealth, alleviating poverty, and promoting the development of SMEs as the backbone of the economy. To achieve this goal, related institutions should innovate delivery channels to increase innovative approaches to enhance financial inclusion. In practice, from the Indonesian experience, the interaction between financial stability and financial inclusion is also being monitored regularly by having various data especially about access not only for the loan or deposit getter from the branch office of the bank or other financial institution, but also for the impact of that loan on the financial stability index. Thus we could measure every single activity making up financial inclusion activity and its impact on the economy as a whole.

In our strategy of financial inclusion, the main goal is to achieve economic welfare through poverty reduction, redistribution of income, and financial systems stability in Indonesia. It can be achieved by creating financial systems that can be accessed by all people in this country at an affordable price.

After removing the bank supervisory function to the Indonesian Financial Service Authority (OJK), the financial inclusion program in Bank Indonesia is being run as part of the financial system stability pillar. Financial system stability is characterized by a strong financial system capable of withstanding economic shock and that is able to ensure intermediary function, settlement of payments, and diversification of risks. So I agree with Peter in this regard, that it is very important to have quantitative research on the impact of financial inclusion on financial stability, because it could help us to define the key performance indicators of financial inclusion activity.

To conclude my comment here, I would suggest three points that are key for the success of financial inclusion for financial stability. The first is a good framework, the second good policy, and the most important thing is good coordination. But there is another "G" that could be considered, which is good luck for financial inclusion activity.

Thank you.

Julius Caesar Parreñas

Peter and Victor have provided us with a very interesting study. And I agree with its conclusions and note that they have rightly pointed out the data limitations that make it difficult to paint a comprehensive picture of the relationship between inclusion and stability. This relationship, as we know, is not a very straightforward one.

Historically, lending to low-income borrowers has been considered by those in the business as low risk. There are many studies using measures such as the ratio of portfolios at risk for more than 30 days, which have pointed to the high quality of microfinance institutions' loan portfolios. The main problem in the beginning for microfinance was high administrative costs. But after these were reduced with the introduction and spread of mobile and agent banking technology, microfinance became very attractive not just to lenders but also to international investors who were attracted by the high quality of assets in combination with geographic diversification, low volatility, and low correlation.

Perceptions changed after Andhra Pradesh in 2010 where high levels of multiple loans taken out by poor people led to over-indebtedness and a crisis of the microfinance sector. The origin of this crisis, of course, lay in an overabundance of credit and competition for lending business, which were fuelled by inflows of public funds and subsidies to nongovernment organizations, and an unprecedented concentration of microfinance institutions in the state.

Nevertheless, it is clear that the problem was not really greater financial inclusion per se, nor increased competition. The problem could be found in the inadequacy of the existing market infrastructure, meaning it could not ensure that lending practices continued to be sound as financial access was expanded. We now know that robust financial education, a better credit information system, and effective consumer protection would have helped prevent the crisis from occurring. I would suspect that if the robustness of the supporting market infrastructure and the quality of the regulatory environment were to be taken into account, the correlation between financial stability and financial inclusion where these conditions are present would be clearly positive.

Fortunately, many governments are becoming aware of these issues and a lot of efforts are being made to address them. The case of Japan, as presented by Mr. Furusawa, illustrates how financial education is being redesigned to build on best practices that underpin the high-level principles and national strategies.

The updated plan for Japan reflects important principles that form the foundations of a successful financial education strategy. The first is, of course, a multi-stakeholder approach that is important for broad support and effectiveness. The second is the view of financial education as a lifelong process that starts with childhood. And the third is a balanced view of the complementary roles of financial education, consumer protection, and expanded financial access in promoting financial innovation and inclusion while preserving stability.

These principles help ensure the effectiveness of the financial education strategy as it is continuously adjusted to achieve the objectives. These are: First, to reflect the constantly changing landscape of financial services, for example the growing popularity of mobile phone and internet banking and the trend toward cross border financial services. Second, to expand the frontiers of financial education, for example to migrant laborers and their families in their home countries or to unbanked rural populations. Third, to find more cost-effective ways of delivering financial education, for example through replacing classroom based models, which are still fairly expensive, with new ones that use technologies that target a narrower selection of customers such as groups of high-value customers, potentially delinquent customers, or other types.

Professor Yoshino's presentation touches on a very important issue that was already discussed in the previous session, which is credit information. We all know that a good credit information system is important for both expanding financial access and ensuring stability. It promotes access because it enables low-income households and small entrepreneurs, who typically do not have physical collateral, to use their reputational collateral, that is, their financial transaction and payment records. This makes it possible for financial institutions to undertake risk-based lending to a larger part of the population. This benefits especially those who are normally discriminated in the absence of financial identity and credit information, such as young people, women in rural areas, and minorities.

Extensive research from various institutions has already confirmed that making more data available to lenders leads to lower default rates and wider lending, including to small businesses. So borrowers benefit from reduced probability of over-extending, fairer prices, reduced credit discrimination, and credit offers that reflect credit risk and credit capacity. Lenders gain better knowledge of borrowers' risk profiles, enabling them to price credit with borrowers appropriately and reduce delinquencies and defaults.

A number of the studies I have mentioned indicate the kind of credit reporting systems that are effective in fulfilling this function, specifically full file systems which include both negative and positive data, and comprehensive systems that include data from different sectors. Of course, the establishment of a system that involves the collection of a wide range of data needs to go hand in hand with the legal and regulatory framework to protect privacy and at the same time to ensure the efficient, permissible use of data.

The importance of credit information for financial inclusion and stability is being increasingly recognized and beginning to be addressed by governments in the region. So we have Japan's credit risk database that Professor Yoshino mentioned and we have other initiatives, for example the PRC's credit reference center under the People's Bank of China that was established in 2006.

Financial inclusion has been successful wherever innovative solutions have been found and applied. We know about mobile phone and agent banking, how they have revolutionized microfinance. We have looked at innovative approaches, like Professor Yoshino's hometown trust funds, how these are being developed in response to behavioral, regulatory, and technological factors that limit the effectiveness of traditional approaches.

In this context, it is important to note that the FSA of Japan, as mentioned by Mr. Furusawa in his presentation, has underscored that government regulations alone can only go so far in achieving user protection, and that excessive regulation could hinder innovation by financial institutions. This is why financial education is very important to ensure that consumers have the capacity to make sound financial decisions that support continued financial stability.

Unfortunately, I only have one minute left, so let me just conclude with a few words on public–private collaboration. Engaging the private sector has become fashionable in this age of limited government resources and the growing needs of society. Indeed, the private sector can contribute significantly to the provision of public goods, including financial education. It is important to point out, however, that the value of public–private partnership lies not only in the added financial resources that can be made available, but also, and probably more importantly, in the additional efficiency that this can inject into projects and initiatives. For this partnership to be effective, however, you need proper frameworks to find the right balance between commercial and public interests that will ensure both continued public support and private sector engagement.

So let me end with this thought, and again thank you very much to the FSA of Japan, ADBI, and IMF for this opportunity to share my personal views.

Open Floor Discussion

Tarisa Watanagase: Thank you very much, JC. While I do not have time to summarize the rich presentations of all the resource persons, I think there are a few "takeaways." Briefly, for financial inclusion you need financial education, you need the reduction of opacity, whether it is opacity in the fee structures, the regulations, or the products. You also need financial infrastructure—specifically, this is Ranee's point that you need to have secured payments systems as well. You need to have credit information innovation.

The next point is that we need to do more studies, more research, and perhaps we need to start with more data on the verification of some stylized facts. This is a point that was made in Peter and Victor's paper. They presented some interesting preliminary results, but again we need to do some more work in that area to challenge or to verify some of the stylized facts about the relationship between financial inclusion and financial stability, and in fact in other areas and on other issues as well.

But most of all, I think that the interesting thing is that this conference has provided a great peer learning opportunity for us to learn from each other how financial inclusion or financial education is being done in different countries. Mr. Furusawa has provided an extensive menu for financial education in Japan, covering all age groups. India is different because the people there seem to be taking higher risks. Maybe that is because of the difference in education or it could be due to the different context of different countries.

So we have a lot of food for thought to take home. Let me open up the floor to the audience. Any questions from the floor?

Participant: Thank you. We heard a lot about government initiatives in the field of financial education. But studies have shown that reinforcing financial education at the time when financial decisions are being made is very important. So my question is, should there be a requirement for financial service providers also to provide neutral inputs at the time when customers are making financial decisions?

Naoyuki Yoshino: In the Japanese case, each financial institution has its own department or section focusing on financial education, because knowledge of how to use those financial products is very important to ensure their products will be understood. So I think not only governments but also each financial institution is participating in this education system.

Tomoyuki Furusawa: I think that is a very important question and I just want to add one point, which is the importance of ethics. I mean that there is some solid conflict of interest between the financial providers and the financial consumers. So we have to establish some ethical code of conduct for the financial institutions as well. We are currently paying more attention to this in close coordination with the Bank of Japan.

Participant: Thank you very much. My question is regarding financial stability and financial inclusion. It was the last point, the six conclusions, where it says that financial inclusion could have both positive and negative implications. The subprime is listed as a negative implication, but my understanding is that if financial inclusion is implemented properly it will keep enhancing the credit standard. So my question to the ADBI team is, what is your ideal definition or background on this issue? Thank you very much.

Peter Morgan: It is likely to lead to higher NPLs, yes, other things being equal. I would certainly agree with the questioner that if inclusion is done properly it should not have negative side effects for financial stability. So the key challenge is to have the regulatory and other frameworks in place that will offset any potential negative impacts.

Participant: I just want to confirm one issue, based on your slide for estimation result two. It says if *fc* and *sfc* have both positive standard errors. Does that mean that in your analysis financial inclusion has positive outcomes for the NPL ratio? Is that correct?

Victor Pontines: Following on from Peter's response. The first bulleted point there in the last slide could actually refer to the stylized facts represented by regressions that were done in the previous slides. But in our technical estimations, when we actually use it to measure financial stability, one is on this bank Z-score, which is a measure of distance of default of commercial banks, which is rated across countries. And regarding nonperforming loans, it turns out to be a positive relationship between other measures of financial inclusion and financial stability. It is what we have got so far, that it is, a positive relation. I am not going to say it is a strong relationship, because of the fact that if you look carefully at the slide it is a very small sample size and again that is due to the data limitations.

So basically the point is, what we are getting in our technical estimation is that because of the diversification aspect of financial inclusion it could actually lead to a lower systemic risk in the financial system. That is what we are getting from the results at the moment.

Tarisa Watanagase: If I may follow up a bit on this issue. I think when we talk about higher NPLs, maybe one does need to look at the risk adjusted between them as well, because smaller entities may have higher risks and they may lead to higher NPLs. But as long as the lending institutions are getting a return which is high enough to cover the risk and the losses, that should be acceptable both for the lending institution and the borrowers. That is my initial thought on this point. So maybe there is some more work to be done for the next piece of the research.

Participant: Thank you for the opportunity. I would like to ask a question regarding the third paper. You pointed out that data scarcity is the main bottleneck for the delay in achieving effective financial inclusion. A great many researchers are always pointing out that drawback and so many times that it always sounds trite. So my question is, is there any commonly accepted requirements, data requirements so to speak, so that the research is considered credible? In other words, what number of observations is acceptable?

Victor Pontines: Well, the more the merrier I guess. So there is really no standard, there is really no exact number of observations, but as a technical answer to a technical question: When you are looking at panel dataset, it should be at least more than a thousand observations. I think that would be the ideal size. So why the limit? Our resources are very much limited because of the very small sample size that we are looking at here. There were two reasons for that. One is because of the scarcity of the data and the very fact that we actually converted the panel dataset into a cross-country regression, which severely limited the number of observations. The reason why we did that is because we just think that on a technical level that reverse causality is a major issue here. I mean, we really want to isolate that direction of relationship in which financial inclusion will actually affect financial stability. We want to isolate that—not the other way around, in which you have financial stability affecting financial inclusion. We just feel that converting to a cross-calculated regression will cause the data problem of reverse causality or endogeneity problems. On the other hand, there is a trade-off involved because of the severity of the sample size. So there is still, as we admitted a while ago, a lot of work to be done on the result, and once we finish the paper we will be switching, I guess, to panel-based estimation. So we will see.

Tarisa Watanagase: Thank you. Unfortunately I think we have to end this session as we have run over time. I would like to invite the audience to give a big hand to the paper presenters and the commentators.

References

Adasme O, Majnoni G, Uribe M (2006) Access and risk: friends or foes? Lessons from Chile. World Bank policy research working paper no. 4003. The World Bank, Washington, DC

Bank of Japan (2013a) Consumer survey on finance, 2013. Bank of Japan, Tokyo, Japan.

Bank of Japan (2013b) Public opinion survey on household financial assets and liabilities, 2013. Bank of Japan, Tokyo, Japan.

European Central Bank (ECB) (2012) Financial stability review. European Central Bank, Frankfurt a. M.

Han R, Melecky M (2013) Financial inclusion for financial stability: access to bank deposits and the growth of deposits in the global financial crisis. World Bank policy research working paper no. 6577. The World Bank, Washington, DC

IMF (2013) Global financial access survey 2013 (2001–2011 avg)

World Bank (2012) Global financial development database (2011 data)

Yoshino N (2012) Global imbalances and the development of capital flows among Asian countries. OECD J Financ Mark Trends 1:81–112

Yoshino N, Kaji S (2013) Hometown investment trust funds: a stable way to supply risk capital. Springer, Tokyo

Session 4: Panel Discussion: Finance to Ensure Asia's Economic Growth

Masahiro Kawai, Muliaman D. Hadad, Mikio Kajikawa, Tarisa Watanagase, Ranee Jayamaha, Hisashi Ono, and Ratna Sahay

Address by Session Chair

Masahiro Kawai

Ladies and gentlemen, this is the last session of the day, Session 4, a panel discussion of Finance to Ensure Asia's Economic Growth. My name is Masahiro Kawai, I am the Dean of the Asian Development Bank Institute, so I think we are going to focus on finance, growth and investment. As you know, in Asia there is a huge potential demand for investment. In particular, infrastructure investment needs are huge. The ADB and ADBI estimated that over the next 10 years, Asia would have to invest at least US$ 750 billion per year for infrastructure investment only.

There are additional investment needs like environmental improvements, disaster risk management, and so forth. Also in the corporate sector, business needs huge

M. Kawai
Asian Development Bank Institute, Tokyo, Japan

M. D. Hadad
Financial Services Authority Indonesia, Jakarta, Indonesia

M. Kajikawa
International Bureau, Ministry of Finance, Tokyo, Japan

T. Watanagase
Bank of Thailand, Bangkok, Thailand

R. Jayamaha
Hatton National Bank PLC, Colombo, Sri Lanka

H. Ono
Supervisory Bureau, Financial Services Agency, Tokyo, Japan

R. Sahay
Monetary and Capital Markets Department, International Monetary Fund, Washington, DC, USA

ADB Institute, Financial Services Agency, Japan, International Monetary Fund Regional Office for Asia and the Pacific (eds.), *Financial System Stability, Regulation, and Financial Inclusion,* ADB Institute Series on Development Economics, DOI 10.1007/978-4-431-55254-3_6

investment—large corporations and SMEs—as was discussed earlier. The household sector also needs investment, in particular mortgage investment, residential investment, and also consumer purchases. The rising middle class are a fluent class and require a substantial amount of investment. So there is a huge need to finance investment in Asia for economic growth.

Unlocking the Small and Medium-Sized Enterprises' Potential to Promote Financial Inclusion and Sustainable Economic Growth

Muliaman D. Hadad

Excellencies, distinguished colleagues, speakers, ladies and gentlemen, good afternoon. First of all, I would like to thank the Financial Services Agency of Japan, ADB Institute, and International Monetary Fund for inviting me to this international conference. I would also like to express my gratitude to the organizers who have organized this conference excellently.

I am very enthusiastic to join all of you in this important event to share, discuss, and gather valuable perspectives from all of you on how to accelerate the development of SMEs. We, as the regulator, certainly need some feedback to help us gain a comprehensive understanding in constructing essential programs to support SMEs development. I believe this panel discussion may provide brilliant ideas that might be of use, not only to authorities, but to anybody who has an interest in this subject.

Before I share my view, let me take some time to tell you about Indonesia FSA's journey in the first year after its establishment. Then I will proceed with my views on how to unlock the potential of micro, small, and medium-sized enterprises to promote better financial inclusion and sustainable economic growth.

It has been a year since the Indonesia FSA, or as we call it, "OJK"—with its dual mandate of supervising the financial sector and providing financial literacy and customer protection—came into operation. 31 December 2012 will be marked as a new era of the Indonesian financial system with the handover of capital market and non-bank financial institutions supervision to OJK. It was a smooth transition, without any unexpected reaction from the market.

Since then we have been building the foundations for being able to conduct an integrated supervision. It is not easy, undoubtedly. As a first step we need to harmonize regulations between sectors in financial industry and set a common standard, based on risk assessment. OJK will enhance the implementation of risk-based supervision of all sectors in the industry. The concept of integrated supervision will be implemented gradually, in line with the aspirations and preparedness of the industry.

Meanwhile, we keep on augmenting supervision of each sector in the industry. In the capital market, we focus on providing a regulatory environment that supports the strengthening and development of the capital market while meeting international standards. As an emerging market, it is really important to have a strong and sound capital market that can work as an alternative to bank finance, especially for long-term investments and infrastructure projects.

We need to speed up the development of our capital markets, both equity and debt markets, including giving small investors and medium-sized enterprises the possibility to utilize the markets. Major initiatives have been taken in developing our capital markets, including simplifying public offering procedures, deepening the stock market, providing an investor protection fund, and developing the bond market. We also have just published a roadmap entitled "Governance Roadmap for Companies in Indonesia: Towards Better Governance of Securities Issuers and Public Companies," which will serve as a role model of governance practice for all companies in Indonesia.

Apart from the capital market, we also prioritize developing the non-bank financial industry in order to lessen the burden of financing borne by banks. Not only that, increasing the number of financially literate middle-income people is in line with higher demand for more financial services such as insurance and pension funds. We cannot be behind the curve. Our young and productive people will turn into ageing societies that might pose social problems in the future. The financial industry would be foolhardy to ignore this fact.

Some major initiatives include creating a Grand Strategy for Micro Insurance, optimizing insurance and reinsurance capacity, establishing an agency for insurance rating and statistics, and increasing the number of actuaries in the insurance and pension fund sectors. OJK has also started preparations for regulating and supervising microfinance institutions, which will commence in 2015. In this regard, we have built a good cooperation with local government bodies throughout the country.

Expanding the contribution of financial services will not be optimal without greater consumer inclusion. Amid the imbalanced bargaining position between customers and financial institutions, the role of consumer education and protection is justified to resolve the problem of asymmetric information. The goal is not only to increase financial literacy, but also to enhance people's financial capability. In this context, OJK has provided Financial Customer Care, as a medium of access to information and dispute resolution between citizens and financial institutions. This is done comprehensively, under the Blueprint of the National Financial Literacy Strategy that we launched in November 2013.

While keeping everything intact, at the same time we also prepared the transition of supervision of the banking sector, the dominant sector in Indonesia's financial system, from the central bank to OJK. Our goal is a smooth transition process that does not have any undesirable impact on the system's stability. To achieve this, we conducted exhaustive and thorough preparations in cooperation with Bank Indonesia.

It was a busy year indeed. So many things to do. We were swamped with work and hardly had time for ourselves. However, the hard work has been worthwhile. The handover of banking regulation and supervision from the central bank to OJK by the end of 2013 occurred smoothly. Banks' business has been unaffected and customers have continued to enjoy banking services. To make sure the banking system continues to function in an orderly fashion, in the initial phase we will maintain the same regulatory regime as before, unless new facts or certain financial market developments make adjustments necessary.

Accordingly, approximately 1200 supervisors from the central bank have been assigned to work with the Indonesia FSA and, simultaneously, 35 FSA offices throughout Indonesia have started to operate. They will play a vital role as the front line for promoting financial literacy and access to finance programs. Most of these offices are still located in the central bank's premises. The Indonesia FSA and the central bank have established excellent cooperation regarding the transfer of human resources, documents, data, and information systems.

I am glad that the establishment of IFSA has had so much support, not only in Indonesia, but also from the international community. Japan's FSA has been one supporter among others. Therefore, I would like to thank Commissioner Hatanaka and the FSA of Japan for the kind assistance they have given us throughout the year.

Another piece of good news is that, just last week, the Indonesia FSA became the 100th signatory to the International Organization of Securities Commissions (IOSCO) Multilateral Memorandum of Understanding on cooperation and exchange information to combat cross-border financial services misconduct. So much has been done. Now let me move to my second topic.

Let me start by quoting Altijana Dzombic, a small business owner in Sarajevo, beneficiary of the World Bank's Enhancing SME Access to Financing Project:

> Production is the future for any country. We need a balance between imports and exports. For 15 years we imported everything...now people have started making [their own goods].

I could not disagree with her testimony. I personally believe that enhancing SMEs goes well beyond poverty alleviation. For most developing countries, SMEs are the backbone of development and quite often they have acted as a shock absorber, as we have seen in many crises we have had to deal with. Even the G20 leaders gave their attention to the critical importance of job creation in the recovery cycle following the recent financial crisis through the promotion of SME development. Clearly, SMEs are not only a developing country phenomenon.

I would like to highlight the important role of SMEs in economic development. SMEs contribute up to 45 % of employment and up to 33 % of GDP in developing economies; these shares are significantly higher when taking into account the estimated contributions of SMEs operating in the informal sector.[1] In Indonesia, this share is even higher.

Taking a closer look at SMEs, everyone agrees that access to finance is a key determinant for business start-ups, and the development and growth of SMEs. However, SMEs have very different needs and face different challenges with regard to financing compared to larger businesses. Large businesses have the option of utiliz-

[1] IFC, Financial Inclusion Experts Group, SME Finance Sub-Group. 2010. Scaling-Up SME Access to Financial Services in the Developing World.

ing capital markets open to them, which is unfortunately not the case for the vast majority of small businesses. Thus, SMEs have to rely solely on bank lending and other types of financial products.

The current economic environment has brought the needs of SMEs into focus. Given the significantly tightened credit supply conditions arising from the reduced ability and willingness of banks to provide the financing on which this sector is particularly reliant, SMEs certainly need alternative sources of financing.

Despite the fact that promoting SME development is an important priority, most countries face almost the same challenges, although with different magnitude, depending on the size of the SME sector. According to an International Finance Corporation (IFC) report, the likelihood of a small firm having access to a bank loan is about a third of what it is for a medium-sized firm, and less than half of what it is for a larger firm. Meanwhile, other sources of finance are still lacking.

Many measures have been taken to open access to finance for SMEs. However, many of these measures have been unsuccessful in terms of addressing market failures. Margaret Hodge, who chairs The Commons Public Accounts Committee in the United Kingdom once said, "Small and medium-sized enterprises have a vital role to play in driving the UK's economic recovery, but despite government attempts to encourage lending to SMEs, many still struggle to access the finance they need."

It is important to keep in mind that SME development projects are not a charity. It is true that they will help to alleviate poverty. But this does not mean that when they have been taken out of poverty, it is the end of SMEs. SMEs will always be there. When the small business has grown into a medium-sized enterprise or even a large enterprise, there will always be a new small business entering the market.

So we cannot just provide these SMEs with a one-time-aid project. We need to construct a generic business model that can be used to provide SMEs with continuous access to finance. It is well known that access to finance is the key. So we simply need to focus on how to tackle this issue. It sounds familiar, but it is really easier said than done.

So, what are we going to do to boost the development of SMEs? Let me echo what IFC has proposed. There are three other important aspects, besides access to finance, which will determine SMEs development.

First, a conducive business environment as the foundation to support SMEs. Regulation is needed to create a favorable investment climate, i.e., simplification of start-up procedures and provision of tax incentives. Solving the regulatory problem is the starting point for SME development.

Second, limited management and operational capacity. We need to focus on capacity building of SMEs through training programs, including financial and marketing aspects and easy access to information. We have to collaborate with other stakeholders such as government, the central bank, and educational institutions to roll out capacity building initiatives to enhance SME competitiveness.

Third, creating linkages between SMEs and large businesses, that can secure the sustainability of SMEs' lines of production. This linkage program proved to be very useful in building managerial and operational capacity.

The final building block, which is of paramount importance, is access to finance. This is a serious challenge for many SMEs that need affordable and tailored credit and investment. We need to think out of the box. We need a breakthrough.

The problem of access for SMEs comes from both demand and supply. On the demand side, most SMEs do not have proper financial accounts, which has consequences. It is hard for financial institutions to make proper evaluations of their financial situations, let alone assessing their business prospects or future cash flows. This is where financial education becomes important. The relevant authorities in Indonesia are working hand in hand to tackle these issues, often also involving the financial industry. We have launched a counseling program on how to create a simple financial report for SMEs. To financial institutions, we have to make them not perceive SME lending as a liability. In fact, when SMEs become bankable, it means more business opportunities. The business outlook of SMEs is very promising. They even dare to borrow from loan-sharks, not just because they do not have access to formal lending, but mostly because they are able to pay the interest.

Education can also help SMEs to get acquainted with financial services. Even though they may know what a bank is, they do not always know how it operates, how to get credit, what the necessary requirements are, etc. Our survey found that even though 57 % of respondents use banking services, only 22 % understand the products. When it comes to financial services providers other than banks, less than 20 % of SMEs surveyed understand the products and their utilization is far smaller. For example, only 2.3 % knows capital markets products and services, and the usage is only 0.1 %.

But survey says that quite a significant proportion of SMEs or people do not understand what services are on offer by banks or financial institutions.

On the supply side, financial institutions are bound by strict regulation. While formal paperwork issues can be tackled through education programs, as I mentioned earlier, the problem of collateral still exists. I can share with you an interesting experience in Indonesia. To tackle the issue of lacking collateral, some of the provincial and local administrations certified people's assets, or more accurately, people's belongings. They certified bicycles, home appliances, and even livestock, which prospective lenders can then use as collateral to get credit. In other places, local governments provide a guarantee scheme by establishing Regional Credit Guarantee Institutions, in order to bring down the risk premium.

Furthermore, we are doing a pilot project to extend the traditional APEX bank in East Java Province. In addition to a guarantee scheme, we are setting up a payment system to enable rural bank customers to make transfers through APEX bank. This pilot project is going quite well and we are now ready to expand the program into other regions.

I am not suggesting relaxation of regulations or direct incentives without solid justification. The development of SMEs must have a business rationale. We need not create any moral hazard. Incentives must be given through market mechanisms. Most importantly, even if there were a generic business model, every country would have to find its own way to match its particular social and cultural environment.

In Indonesia, several banks have been pioneers in financing for SMEs. I observe that these businesses are doing very well as more and more banks these days are keen to enter SME financing. This is proof that SME business is promising.

Before I conclude my speech, I would like to convey my great belief that East Asia should be the leader in finding sustainable SMEs programs, since almost half of the world's SMEs are in East Asia. We need to create more and more initiatives to make them grow, not just for their sake. We all need sound and well-functioning SMEs to provide jobs, to preserve the financial system, for macroeconomic stability, and to guarantee a balanced and sustainable growth. Thank you.

Presentations by Panelists

Mikio Kajikawa

Thank you Chairman. My name is Mikio Kajikawa from the Finance Ministry. My job is covering IMF issues and G20 issues, and actually I am G20 Deputy Director-General of the Ministry of Finance and I attend all the G20 meetings. I just returned from Canada to attend one of the meetings and it was less than 20 °F there. Now I am feeling rather warm here in Tokyo. But many participants are from the southern countries, so I hope you are enjoying what is a very cold winter in Tokyo I think. Thank you for the invitation and I think my job here is to add something from the macro side of the stability issues.

Last year, I attended many G20 meetings and one of the stability issue discussed there was about tapering and reactions to it. Everything started on 22 May, when Chairman Bernanke announced that he will start to taper. After that, even though tapering was not started at that time, we observed the market turbulence of July and August last year. On 18 September, the Federal Open Market Committee (FOMC) decided not to begin to taper in September. After that, the markets stabilized somewhat. On 18 December of last year, the FOMC finally decided to start tapering from January 2014. Despite the announcement, the market remained fairly stable. This is the background of the discussion.

What we observed is that some countries were very, very resilient to this tapering announcement. The currencies of the Republic of Korea and the PRC in fact appreciated. The currencies of some countries, like Thailand, India, Brazil, Turkey, and Indonesia, depreciated (Table 1). This may be related to some of the countries' fundamentals. For example, the Republic of Korea and the PRC are running a current account surplus, which makes their currencies more stable I think.

We have been discussing this issue again and again in the G20 and finally reached a conclusion, which is stated in G20 communique last October. For emerging markets, some macroeconomic policies, structural reforms, and strong prudential frameworks will help support an increase in productivity. For advanced economies,

Table 1 Economic situations in emerging markets

	Appreciation/depreciation of local currency (%)	Current account to GDP (%)	CPI (%)
Rep. of Korea	4.8	3.8	2.2
People's Rep. of China	1.4	2.3	2.6
Thailand	▲9.1[▲9.6]	0.0	3.0
India	▲9.9[▲19.4]	▲4.8	10.4
Brazil	▲13.1[▲16.5]	▲2.4	5.4
Turkey	▲15.6[▲15.6]	▲6.1	8.9
Indonesia	▲19.2[▲20.3]	▲2.7	4.3

Appreciation/Depreciation of local currency: Last price change from 22 May 2013 to 15 Jan 2014 ([ ] means lowest level since 22 May 2013.)
Current Account and CPI: Actual number of 2012 by IMF World Economic Outlook published in Oct 2013

which are running unconventional monetary policies, the statement says that we will ensure that future changes of monetary policy settings will continue to be carefully calibrated and clearly communicated. Calibration and communication are important, that is what we agreed on at the G20.

The next point is about Asia. Even though we observed some market turbulence last year, I think Asian economies are more resilient because of our experience of the Asian market crisis. This resilience comes from four layers (Table 2). The first is foreign reserves, the second is bilateral financial cooperation, the third is regional financial cooperation, and the last is more directed to the IMF.

On the first point, before the crisis foreign reserves were limited, but after the crisis, I think, many Asian countries accumulated a lot of foreign reserves. For example, in Indonesia foreign reserves were US$ 16.6 billion before the crisis, but now they have more than US$ 108 billion in foreign reserves. This is just one example, but I can say that the Asian countries are now accumulating a lot of foreign reserves.

The second layer is bilateral financial cooperation, namely bilateral currency swap arrangements (BSAs) and the structuring of the framework to provide local currencies. Japan is now making BSAs with many of the Asian countries and that will be of help if something happens in this market.

Thirdly, regional financial cooperation, and with that I mean the Chiang Mai Initiative. We already agreed that the size of the Chiang Mai Initiative will be doubled from US$120 billion to US$ 240 billion and we also set up an ASEAN+3 Macroeconomic Research Office (AMRO), and this is headed by our friend Mr. Nemoto. This is the third area of close regional financial cooperation.

And lastly, IMF. Before the Asian crisis, the IMF set up very broad conditionality and access is limited to 100% of quotas. But the IMF has already streamlined the conditionality and doubled the access limit and now we have a new lending scheme, the flexible credit line (FCL), and so on, so now I think the Asian countries are more resilient to the crisis.

Table 2 Asian financial safety net: before/after the Asian currency crisis. (Source: Ministry of Finance)

	Before the crisis	After the crisis
1. Foreign reserves[a]	Limited foreign reserves (Total reserves, total reserves in months of imports (1997))	Abundant foreign reserves (Total reserves, total reserves in months of imports (2012))
	Indonesia: US$ 16.6 billion, 3.9	Indonesia: US$ 108.8 billion, 6.8 (6.6, 1.7 times larger than in 1997)
	Malaysia: US$ 20.8 billion, 3.2	Malaysia: US$ 137.8 billion, 8.4 (6.6, 2.6 times larger than in 1997)
	Thailand: US$ 26.2 billion, 5.0	Thailand: US$ 173.3 billion, 8.3 (6.6, 1.7 times larger than in 1997)
2. Bilateral financial cooperation		Bilateral currency swap arrangements (BSAs) with Asian countries India, Indonesia, Philippines, etc
		Structuring the framework to provide local currencies
		Cross-border collateral arrangements utilizing JGB as collateral between central banks, etc
3. Regional financial cooperation		ASEAN+3 Regional financial cooperation
		Chiang Mai Initiative Multilateralization (CMIM) (US$ 120 billion → US$ 240 billion)
		ASEAN+3 macroeconomic research office (AMRO)
		Asian bond markets initiative (ABMI)
4. IMF	Broad conditionality	Streamlined conditionality
	Narrow access limit	Doubled access limit:
	100 % of Quota(annual)[a]	200 % of Quota(annual)[a]
	300 % of Quota(cumulative)[a]	600 % of Quota(cumulative)[a]
	[a]In case of stand-by arrangement (SBA)/extended fund facility (EFF)	New Lending instruments e.g., Flexible Credit Line (FCL) enables qualified countries to draw at any time within a pre-specified window on the credit line, or to treat it as a precautionary instrument with no ongoing conditions

[a]IMF

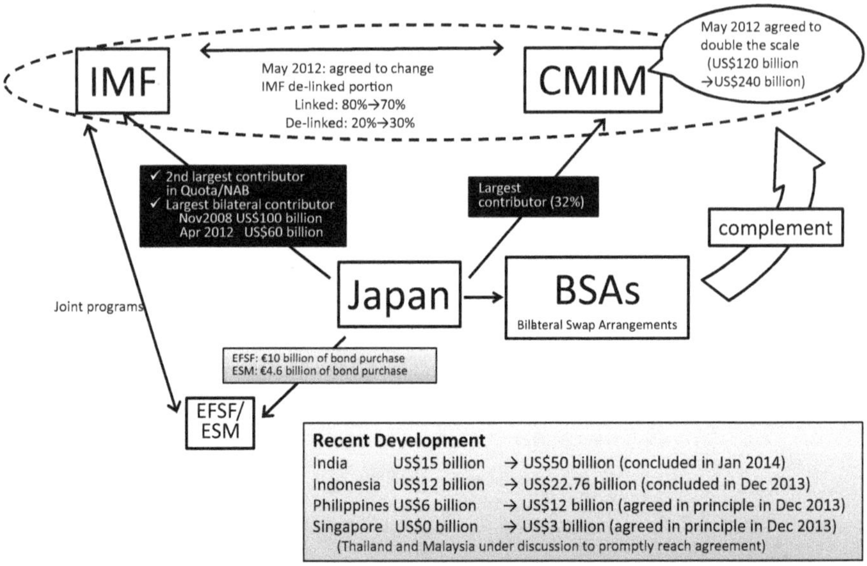

Fig. 1 Japan's contribution to the global financial safety net. (Source: Ministry of Finance)

Japan is contributing to all the layers (Fig. 1). For example we are the second largest contributor to the IMF and we are the largest contributor to the Chiang Mai Initiative, with 32% of the Chiang Mai amount. Recently, we have developed BSAs. We just agreed with India that the BSA will be increased from US$ 15 billion to US$ 50 billion. With Indonesia and the Philippines, we decided to double the amount of the BSA, and for Singapore we restarted the arrangement from US$ 0 to US$ 3 billion. This is the Japanese contribution to financial stability in Asian countries.

This slide shows capital flows from Japan to Asian countries (Fig. 2). The left-hand side is outstanding loans of Japanese banks to Asia and the right-hand side is foreign direct investment from Japan to Asia—both are increasing. When we started the very unconventional monetary policy, Japan's so-called Quantitative and Qualitative Monetary Easing, some argued that this may bring some very risky money into Asian markets. But in fact, we increased bank loans as well as foreign direct investment, which contribute to the growth of Asia.

To conclude, I would like to state three points. The first point is about the G20. We are working hard to tackle the issue of market stabilization. The second point is that Asia is becoming more resilient to market crises because of these four layers: reserves, bilateral, regional, and multilateral. The third point is that Japan is supporting the Asian countries through the government as well as the private sector. We contribute a lot to multilateral and bilateral arrangements, and Japanese private money is supportive to Asian growth.

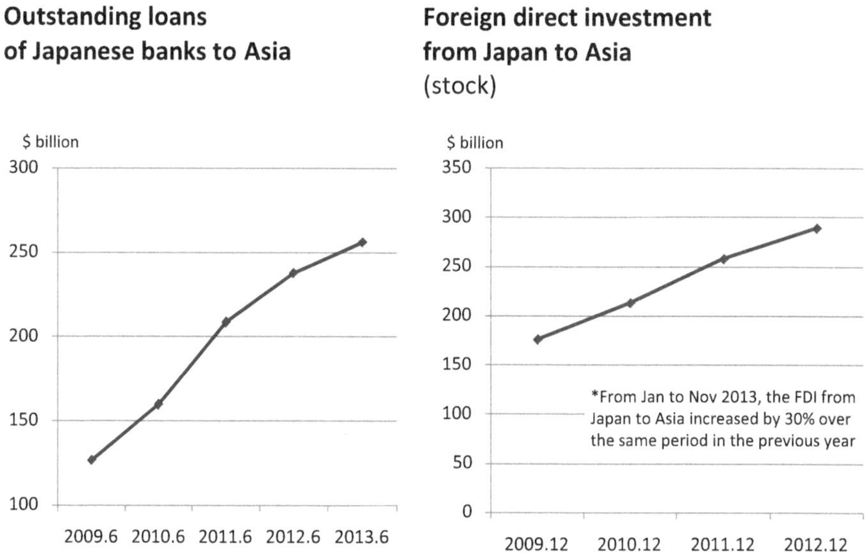

Fig. 2 Capital flow. (Sources: *Left*, Bank for International Settlements; *Right*, Japan External Trade Organization and Ministry of Finance, Japan)

Tarisa Watanagase

Thank you, Dean Kawai. I would like to offer my thoughts on two areas: first on financial inclusion, which is an issue that we have been discussing since the morning, and also follow up with my thoughts on the issue of financing to ensure Asia's growth.

On the area of financial inclusion, there is work that needs to be done and there are several players that have to be involved. I would like to talk about these roles of different players to see a clearer picture of what needs to be done.

The first player would be the combination of the financial institutions and the regulators. They need to make efforts to build up financial infrastructure and environments. Some of these issues were discussed earlier. For example, we need to have credit information, we need to have a secured e-payment system, a secure settlement system, and also we need them to work closely together in order to try to develop some of the credit substitutes such as leasing, factoring, and even venture capital. These are substitutes that can help out the SMEs and lead to further financial inclusion.

The second player would be the regulators. Regulations must keep up with evolving technology and the new players. Regarding technologies like e-payment, we need to develop communication technology. And as new players, of course, we very clearly see the increasing role of the telephone companies. What do we do with them? How can they be regulated? And at the same time, their role and the evolving technology must also be encouraged to enable more cost-effective ways of delivery.

The next area for regulators is that they need to make sure that the global standard is proportionate with regards to financial inclusion. You probably know that the G20 in 2010 encouraged the standard setting bodies to try to encourage financial inclusion in a way that is consistent with their mandates such as financial stability in the case of BCBS and anti-money laundering and counter-terrorism financing in the case of FATF. These global standard setters have issued guidelines for financial inclusion. Fortunately, most standard setters seem to have a good understanding that the risks of financial inclusion product providers and transactions are very different from that of the traditional formal sector of the financial institution and standards for financial inclusion need to be proportionate to its magnitude of risks. Specifically, loans to small borrowers and to SMEs have a very different magnitude of systemic risk because of the small size of the loan. So if the standard for supervisors of financial inclusion service providers requires that they comply with the Basel Core Principles for bank supervision in the same way as the supervision of traditional financial institutions, it can have the unintended consequences of leading, in fact, to further financial exclusion, rather than inclusion. Since financial inclusion is very diverse, with different implementations, practices and contexts, supervisors need to learn from each other how supervision is done in different countries and engage with the standard setting bodies so that they learn from these diverse experiences of developing countries and keep their guidelines adequately proportionate and in line up with this diversity.

The third player would be the government. I think the government needs to work on the collateralization of movable collaterals simply because the SMEs do not have that much immovable collateral. This will certainly enhance credit quality. They need to establish the registries and then also formally declare creditor rights and the hierarchy of rights as well to movable collaterals in case there is a default.

Governments can do the credit guarantee or do direct financing, but it is important to bear in mind that they have to prevent moral hazard. So there must be a sensible way of sharing risk among all the parties involved and that means the borrowers, the lending institutions, and the government agency that is providing either credit guarantees or direct financing.

The next thing that we need to do is financial education. This is not a player, but it is an issue that we need to take into account. On the issue of financial inclusion, there are papers that discuss not just what to do in financial education, but also how to deliver financial education. There is a paper that I came across by Cho and Honerati in 2013. They presented some empirical study—for example, one of the studies is that vocational and business training in fact works better than financial training and the impact can be further enhanced if the vocational and business training are combined with financing or counseling. So I would encourage more research into these areas, not just into education, but, as I said earlier, into modifying the stylized facts with a view to enriching our tools, enriching our wisdom, in order to bring about more financial education and financial inclusion.

With that, I would like to move on to the issue of financing to ensure Asia's growth. The first point I would like to make is that Asian banks are doing relatively well in supporting their countries' growth. Because unlike Wall Street—Wall Street has a disconnect between financial activity and the real sector economy—with the connection to the real sector that we see in the Asian banks, I think I will be less worried about this role of the Asian banks. So they should keep on doing this and they should keep on focusing on this role of supporting the real economy.

Of course, regarding the big corporations, Dean Kawai mentioned earlier the need for finance, especially in the area of infrastructure. Being big, they can have direct access to both the stock markets and bond markets, whether they are domestic markets or international markets. We also heard from our earlier speaker that there are already a number of regional initiatives in place to promote that—the Chiang Mai Initiative for example and the bond market development program in Asia. Of course, the governments in individual countries will have to further deepen their stock markets and bond markets in order to support this role of Asian banks of financing the real economy.

The second point is that the supervisors are generally ensuring that the banking sector is supporting the real economy. And just like supervisors and central banks in the developed economies, supervisors and central banks in developing countries too play a role in supporting SMEs, while also playing more of a developmental role. So there is good cooperation between the banking sector and the supervisor. All in all, I would say that they are doing a relatively good job in supporting growth.

Obviously, there are concerns on the issue of efficiency and stability. Regarding the issue of efficiency, this is something that we need to look into more closely. What measure do we use to measure efficiency? Do we look at, for example, the cost-to-income ratio, or do we look at the price that the customer pays? There are weaknesses in using these measures for cross-country comparisons, because this can reflect different risks. For example, cost–income can reflect different income structures in different countries. But without going further into the details, I think I would definitely agree that efficiency is an issue. In the case of Thailand, cost-to-income ratio is still relatively high and there certainly is room for reduction. But learning from the 1997 crisis, I would strongly agree with what Ranee said this morning, that sequencing is very important and getting the sequencing right is crucially important. I mean, you need to develop and increase the resilience of the financial sector before you can actually open it up to more competition.

The next point is about stability. That is the last point I want to make. Again, I think Asian banks are generally resilient after the Asian crisis. They generally have a high level of capital and low risk and they are also very much risk-focused. That is why they were able to escape the adverse impact of the global crisis relatively well. Supervisors are also doing a much better job. They have improved their supervision and their inspection, also since 1997. They are very much risk-focused on both micro and macro stability issues, using various tools, not just the traditional ones, but also macro prudential tools and also stress tests. And they have also introduced, or are in the process of introducing, global standards.

I may have sounded very optimistic, but of course the Asian banks have weaknesses, especially in the area of financial stability. I think the Asian banks have a tendency to move to financial imbalances. In other words, I think they are prone to financial imbalances and this is because of a few factors. First of all, most developing economies are small and they also have shallow financial markets. Therefore, it is difficult for them to adjust to global shocks. Secondly, they usually have a short spectrum of financial assets available for investment, so there are not that many choices for the investors and savers, and there is a tendency for bubbles to build up in their stock markets and property markets. Especially in the property markets, we tend to have inadequate data or information on critical indicators, such as property prices and the number of houses being built, the remaining stocks, and things like that.

So these are the areas that we need to pay attention to. Thank you very much.

Ranee Jayamaha

Thank you again. Dr. Tarisa took us through the details on financial inclusion and education and I will try to avoid repetition in the interest of time.

Asia Will Continue to Be the Growth Center in the Next Few Years

According to the OECD Development Centre's Medium-Term Projection Framework and the World Bank's economic outlook, Emerging Asia (Southeast Asia, the PRC, and India) is projected to grow by a moderate 6.9 % over the medium term (2014–2018), based on a steady rise in domestic demand. In the ASEAN group, growth will remain robust at an average of 5.4 % per annum in the same period (Table 3).

This slower pace largely reflects the moderation of growth in the PRC (7.7 %) and India (5.9 %) in 2013.

The GDP growth projections for individual countries reflect their different stages of development and medium-term growth drivers. Indonesia is projected to be the fastest-growing economy within the ASEAN 6, with an average annual growth rate of 6.0 % in 2014–2018. The strong medium-term economic outlook for Indonesia and the Philippines (5.8 %) will be underpinned by steady growth in domestic demand, strong infrastructure spending, and implementation of structural reforms.

Led by the rising growth in domestic demand, especially in infrastructure, investment and private consumption, real GDP in Malaysia and Thailand is projected to grow by an average annual rate of 5.1 and 4.9 %, respectively, during 2014–2018. Whether these growth rates would be sufficient for Malaysia and Thailand to overcome the middle-income trap is debatable.

Singapore is projected to grow by 3.3 % per annum during this period. The rate of growth reflects the country's more advanced stage of economic development. The Singapore economy is moving towards more sustainable, inclusive growth led by increases in productivity and innovation.

The CLMV countries (Cambodia, Lao PDR, Myanmar, and Viet Nam) are projected to grow at a higher pace over the medium term, led by Lao PDR at 7.7 % per annum. Real GDP growth in Cambodia and Myanmar is projected to average

Table 3 Real GDP growth of Southeast Asia, the PRC, and India (annual % change). (Source: OECD Development Centre, MPF-2014)

	2012	2018	2014–2018	2000–2007
ASEAN 6 countries				
Brunei Darussalam	1.0	2.4	2.3	n.a.
Indonesia	6.2	6.1	6.0	5.1
Malaysia	5.6	5.3	5.1	5.5
Philippines	6.8	5.9	5.8	4.9
Singapore	1.3	3.1	3.3	6.4
Thailand	6.5	5.3	4.9	5.1
CLMV countries				
Cambodia	7.2	7.1	6.8	9.6
Lao PDR	7.9	7.5	7.7	6.8
Myanmar	n.a.	7.0	6.8	n.a.
Viet Nam	5.2	6.0	5.4	7.6
Average of ASEAN 10	5.5[a]	5.6	5.4	5.5[b]
2 large economies in Emerging Asia				
PRC	7.7	7.5	7.7	10.5
India	3.7	6.1	5.9	7.1
Average of Emerging Asia	6.4	6.9	6.9	8.6

Emerging Asia = ASEAN 10 countries plus the PRC and India

PRC People's Republic of China, *ASEAN* Association of Southeast Asian Nations, *CLMV* Cambodia, Lao PDR, Myanmar, and Viet Nam, *Lao PDR* Lao People's Democratic Republic, *n.a.* not available

[a]excluding Myanmar

[b]excluding Brunei Darussalam

close to 7% in 2014–2018. These countries are opening up to foreign investment. As for Viet Nam, its real GDP is projected to remain robust in the medium term, but growth will be slower than prior to the global financial crisis because of slower external demand from advanced economies and weak macroeconomic management policies. Outside this league, Sri Lanka is becoming a fast growing middle-income country with a growth forecast of 7.0–7.5% in 2014–2018 and is aspiring to reach middle-income country status.

The PRC's real GDP growth is expected to moderate to around 7.7% in 2014–2018 (compared with 10.5% during 2000–2007), as the country rebalances its growth strategy to be based on domestic consumption. Implementation of structural reforms will also be critical in driving the PRC economy toward sustainable development and growing beyond the middle-income trap. The slowdown in the PRC in particular could weaken the growth momentum of Southeast Asian economies, as the PRC a key trading partner of these economies. At the same time, India's growth is expected to moderate to 5.9% in 2014–2018, compared with 7.1% in 2000–2007.

Asia Will Continue to Demand Resources to Sustain Its Growth Momentum and Investment Growth Will Remain Robust

Investment is projected to remain robust in Emerging Asia over 2014–2018, at 6.6 % per annum. In the Southeast Asia region, investment growth is projected to be healthy in the next 5 years, at 6.3 % per annum, with higher demand for investment in Indonesia and the Philippines, which are projected to grow at a faster pace compared with others. Investment growth in the PRC and India is projected to moderate during 2014–2018, due to structural adjustments and budgetary issues as well as uncertainties over prospects for further reforms.

Although markets are expected to be less liquid than in 2013, there are various new avenues of investment flows into Asia in 2014. North Asia (Japan; the Republic of Korea; and Taipei,China) and Singapore (South Asia) will attract investment with their conducive investment environments and good banking and financial services. Authorities in South Asia have also relaxed their exchange control procedures and opened up capital markets, while some are striving for fully opened capital market status. Compared with the US and Europe, inflation rates in Asia are still high, so real interest rates will continue to be positive for some time.

Financing Asia's Growth

There are a number of sources that can be tapped to finance Asia's growth, but Asia needs to make significant efforts to secure funding in a challenging environment.

Except North Asia, the Republic of Korea, Japan where savings ratios are high, the other countries are not able to fund Asia's growth through their savings as many of them are plagued by the twin deficits (budget and current account deficits) and are constrained in their ability to fill the savings and investment gap. This is certainly the case for Sri Lanka, Viet Nam, and India.

The growing new rich in India and the PRC would be looking around for short- and long- term investment opportunities in emerging Asia. Emerging South Asia (Nepal, Sri Lanka, and Bangladesh) and South East Asia (Lao PDR and Viet Nam) should make efforts to attract investment from the new rich in India and the PRC.

Given their relatively strong macroeconomic fundamentals and narrow savings and investment gaps, North Asia, i.e., Japan; the Republic of Korea; Taipei,China; and Singapore (South Asia) are relatively less affected by external factors and they are still attractive to foreign investors. Some Asian countries do not have large projects to attract foreign direct investment and foreign portfolio investment. These countries are also suffering from large debt deficits and have created uncertainties for (potential) foreign investors. At the same time, Japan and the Republic of Korea are seeking investment opportunities in large-scale infrastructure projects in emerging Asian countries such as Bangladesh, Sri Lanka, and Viet Nam. Reduction in capital flows: projections for 2014–2016 capital flows to developing countries are predicted to be revised downwards due to a gradual tightening of the quantitative easing program and a modest recovery in the developed countries. In July 2013, money and capital markets in Indonesia, India, and to some extent Malaysia, Sri Lanka, and many other countries, suffered as a result of the US Federal Reserve's initial announcement of the tapering off of quantitative easing through a reduction in the bond buying program. Many currencies (in particular the Indian rupee and the Indonesian rupiah) plunged to very low levels in the third quarter of 2013. Flight to quality was attributable to the twin deficits and the high debt burden in Asia.

Against this background, South Asia will retain and will be able to secure a part of the funds which are already invested in short- to medium-term financial assets. For example, even as recent as the beginning of January 2014, Sri Lanka raised US$ 1 billion for 5 years, which was three times oversubscribed with US investors taking up more than two thirds of the sovereign debt, while Indonesia and the Philippines have raised sovereign debt at even finer rates.

2014 may not see the same surge experienced in the last 2 years, but it is expected that regional and global banks will meet part of the loan demand for corporates in Asia, implying significant primary issuance over the next few years. Following the near full capital account liberalization (Sri Lanka) where big banks as well as corporates are allowed to borrow from international markets on their own credentials, foreign borrowing by emerging middle-income countries will increase.

The Middle-Income Trap

In recent years, the attention of scholars and policymakers has turned to explaining how and why most middle-income countries have failed to make the transition to high-income status. This failure has been called the "middle-income trap" (Gill and Kharas 2007). It refers to a developmental stage characterized by a slowdown in growth patterns (Latin American) inability to move up the value chain, away from factor-driven, export-dependent growth and into new innovation-driven industries.

More recently, a large number of low-income countries have succeeded in escaping the poverty trap and joined the ranks of a broad group of middle-income countries, but only a few, notably Japan, the Republic of Korea, Singapore, Israel, and Ireland, have sustained their development progress and transformed themselves into high-income countries.

Some evidence suggests that developing countries become vulnerable to the growth slowdown characteristic of the middle-income trap at two stages: first around a per capita income of US$ 10,000–US$ 11,000 and again around US$ 15,000–US$ 16,000 (at purchasing power parity exchange rates and 2005 prices). Some have argued, however, that the middle-income trap can occur around a per capita income of US$ 5,000–US$ 6,000.

Some observers have questioned whether the growth slowdowns associated with the middle-income trap can be viewed as a "trap" in any meaningful sense.

However, whether the term "trap" or another term is used, the fact remains that many middle-income countries have found it difficult to sustain their development progress, which points to the overriding challenge now faced by many of the emerging countries.

Strengthening the Financial System to Support Development Beyond the Middle-Income Trap

The success of Emerging Asia in avoiding the middle-income trap will critically depend upon the capabilities of these countries' financial systems. In the coming years, their financial systems will have to meet several challenges:

- Credit will need to be channeled efficiently and on financially sound terms to sectors and businesses leading the transformation of the economy, which will often be different, or have different characteristics, from those where credit has traditionally gone;
- Financial institutions will need to have the capabilities and incentives to operate as commercial entities and the ability to sustain sound lending and risk management practices;
- Financial instruments and services will need to be developed to meet the needs of SMEs, the growing middle class, aging populations, rural households, and other population segments that are now underserved, to ensure that growth is inclusive;
- Financial regulatory and supervisory systems will need to be capable of containing risks to avoid system instability that can arise from rapidly changing domestic and international economic conditions;
- Domestic financial systems will need to adapt to, and accommodate, growing linkages to regional and international financial markets.

The economies of Emerging Asia have made considerable progress since the 1997–1998 Asian financial crisis in reforming their financial systems to meet these challenges. Probably the most important accomplishment has been the strengthening of prudential norms and of financial regulatory and supervisory capabilities. The fruits of these reforms could be seen in the generally much stronger financial positions of banks during the 2007–2009 global financial crisis. Significant progress has also been made in the strengthening of BFIs, to enable them to focus on efficiency and competitiveness.

BFIs in emerging Asia should now look at enhancing financial inclusion, and financial education and literacy as the upcoming SMEs have to be protected from internal and external vulnerabilities. The situation requires concentrated action by all stakeholders.

- Efficiency and competition in banking systems are still limited in some countries, owing in part to restrictions on private sector or foreign participation.

- Capital markets, especially bond markets, are comparatively underdeveloped, perpetuating the high dependence on and concentration of financial risk in the banking system, thus limiting the financial options available to borrowers and savers.
- Diversity and sophistication of financial instruments and services, such as consumer credit, derivatives for managing risks, and vehicles for longer-term investment, including infrastructure development and post retirement savings, are still limited.
- Some segments of the population as well as businesses—notably SMEs—are presently underserved in terms of their overall access to credit and financial services.

Development of domestic capital markets: While money market contributions will become tight, driven by Basel III and other regulations, Asia should focus on capital market development to attract long-term bonds, debentures, and stock market investments. The governance structures of capital markets should be improved while encouraging debt issuance to introduce innovative products in local or foreign currencies to attract foreign funds. Countries should also encourage IT BPO/KPO and PPP ventures to facilitate joint ventures and foreign investments. Depending on the macroeconomic condition, countries need to consider opening local treasury bills and bond markets to enable foreigners to invest up to tolerable levels and issue foreign currency denominated bills and bonds to attract investors. In this regard, the authorities should be mindful of the "hot money" nature of inflows and be ready to face consequences as and when investors pull out for numerous reasons.

Encourage regional and private equity funds to be set up in emerging Asian countries. International financial institutions like ADB and IFC need to consider providing guarantees to fundraising countries.

Financial Inclusion/Education

India's economy has developed at a rapid pace in the last decade, thereby improving the living standards of people and encouraging growth sectors using information and communication technology (ICT). Sri Lanka has been focusing on financial education and inclusion for some time and has been moderately successful in this effort.

Emerging Asia has made remarkable progress over the past 4 decades in raising income levels, reducing poverty, developing manufacturing, investing in partnerships and business relationships, and developing agency links between investors and entrepreneurs.

Government policies will be crucial in determining the success of the middle-income ASEAN countries, the PRC, and India, in orienting their economic and industrial structures towards sustainable growth. Similarly, using a diverse set of tools and gateways (payments systems), financial inclusion should be promoted. Historical experience—e.g., the success stories of Japan, the Republic of Korea, and Singapore—underscores the importance of focusing policies on building and strengthening institutions which supply key ingredients needed for industrial transformation and shape business incentives and the ability to respond to changing market conditions and opportunities.

Institutional development will be the key to success in achieving desired results. Educational and other institutions provide human capital, foster innovation, and facilitate infrastructure development, but they are typically weaker in developing countries than in advanced economies as are legal and regulatory frameworks for competition, corporate governance, and business entry and exit, and they need to be strengthened if development is to be sustained. In many Emerging Asian countries (Sri Lanka, Bangladesh) and others, implementing regulatory reforms to reduce barriers to SMEs and developing the services sector have a high priority.

The need to improve access to education and strengthen education and vocational training institutions is especially acute in Indonesia and Thailand, while Malaysia focuses on strengthening links between academic and research institutions and industry. Japan has been more successful in this field than others. The PRC and Viet Nam need to facilitate the development of the private sector and better define the involvement of state-owned businesses in the economy, although the PRC is much further ahead in this transition.

Impact of Basel III on Credit Growth of Banks Will Be Significant in Asia at a Time When Credit Is Vital

It appears that Basel III will have a significant impact on the composition of credit markets in the region, causing banks to increase their share of corporate funding at the expense of loans to retailers over the next decade. Banks are also likely to deploy their increasingly scarce funding resources in a more capital-efficient manner.

Basel III is a strong step forward in the global efforts to minimize banking risks. As different jurisdictions have adopted different phases of implementation and national treatments, it is difficult to know whether there already is a level playing field and the consequences on different economies are unclear. There is a further risk that "one-size-fits-all" rules may add to systemic fragility because the diversity of systems adds to overall global systemic stability. It is the willingness to experiment with different types of macro-prudential tools and structural reforms in combination with Basel III rules that holds the key to addressing the different conditions and risks confronting national regulators.

Going forward, Asian regulators can do more to balance financial regulation and real sector needs. The implementation of Basel III in Asia needs to be placed in a proper context to ensure that the new standards are complied with and where possible suit domestic conditions.

To achieve financial system stability, there is a need to look holistically at real sector imbalances, monetary and fiscal policies, and interconnectivity and feedback mechanisms between the financial institutions (including shadow banks) and the real economy as a whole.

Hisashi Ono[2]

Thank you, Dean Kawai. I would like to make three comments. The first one concerns support for SMEs. As Dr. Muliaman pointed out, SMEs are profitable, and supporting and nurturing SMEs are basic roles for financial institutions. Therefore, financial institutions should provide support for SMEs, not only in financial terms, but also in other management challenges, such as boosting sales.

Having said that, there might be limitations to some degree for financial institutions to provide support to SMEs by themselves. Therefore, the utilization of outside organizations and experts would be effective for financial institutions, especially to provide advice for boosting sales. However, the problem is how to find an adequate outside organization and experts. At the Japanese FSA, we are now tackling this very important and very difficult issue, how to organize the system so that adequate outside organizations and experts could be provided for SMEs which are at different stages and facing difficult challenges. This is one of the challenges.

The second comment regards equity financing to SMEs. Not only provision of loans, but also equity financing is indispensable for SMEs, especially on the enterprises which are at the start-up stage. The problem is how and from where such risk capital will be raised. We should make various efforts to raise risk capital, for example diversification of financing methods such as methods for the provision of causal equity, transformation of personal funds into capital, and opening up new negotiation channels, such as nurturing micro investor funds and crowd funding. This is my second comment.

The last one regards financial inclusion. I think it is necessary to strengthen the links between academia, research institutions, and the financial services industry. In this respect, the Japanese FSA, in full collaboration with other ministries, has been making efforts to strengthen collaboration among industry, academia, finance, and government. A private–public body called the Local Roundtable, composed of representatives of industry, universities, financial institutions, and local governments in the region, has already been established.

Such a local roundtable has been established in several local areas to exchange information and opinions and discuss how to revitalize local economies and to promote new industry in the region.

At the end, I would like to close with a few words of Professor Shiller of Yale University who, as you know, is a Nobel Prize winner. He said that finance is one of the most powerful tools we have for solving our common problems and increasing the general well-being. He said, financial innovation and finance should play a large role in helping society achieve its goals. I fully agree with his words. We should continue to make further efforts to think about how to utilize financial instruments in broader terms to support SMEs in Asia.

Thank you.

[2] The views expressed in this presentation are those of the author and do not necessarily reflect the views of the Financial Services Agency or the FSA Institute.

Ratna Sahay

Thank you, Dr. Kawai. I will also try to be very brief. I would like to make two broad points. First, where should Asia's financial sector head? Where should it go? Second, as we look forward, what challenges do you think it is going to face?

On the first point, we all know that maintaining Asia's rapid growth and increasing investment, especially in infrastructure, will require addressing Asia's structural challenges. So let me just point to three. These are not new and many speakers have talked about it. First, diversifying away from bank financing. This is going to be very important. Developing bond markets as instruments to complement longer term bank lending is going to be critical. A second area is going to be to provide greater and diversified opportunities for saving, and here Dr. Yoshino's chart was very revealing when it compared the US with Japan for example. This will also support the Asian populations' niche. A third area—and a lot that was said in this conference relates to this—is increasing financial inclusion in Asia. As a matter of fact, when we look at the data, we see that Asia lags other regions in inclusiveness. Here the charts by Peter Morgan and Victor Pontines on financial inclusion and GDP levels, which show very strong relations, are quite striking.

Extending banking and insurance services is important, but just because there was so much emphasis on SME lending, let me make one major point on SME lending. To me it is not critical and in fact sometimes it could lead to adverse results if you provide guarantees or direct lending and, in fact, in many countries like India and the PRC there are also implicit guarantees. To me that is not critical.

To me the critical thing is that the SMEs should have a level playing field, the same playing field as big banks. But right now there is an implicit subsidy for the really big banks that needs to go. So, how else can you improve the level playing field? And many speakers have talked about improving the market infrastructure, about financial education, and about credit bureaus providing non-financial information. So the main point I want to make is, it is about providing a level playing field.

The second point is about what challenges Asia is going to face as financial markets evolve and develop. First, as capital account liberalization will take place because many economies are not fully liberalized and there is going to be rising regional integration, there are many lessons that we can learn from the recent Global Financial Crisis. The first is the need to improve cross-border regulatory coordination, and you can have a head start. You can start doing it from now. Second, there are also going to be increasing interconnectedness and complex financial sectors and financial innovation which will create new markets, but it will also bring in new risks. Again, this requires looking ahead and developing prudential oversight and a strong focus on capital and derivative markets and shadow banking. Again, this region can do that starting now. Finally, there are also lessons to be learned on the crisis resolution framework. In fact, focusing on crisis resolution frameworks, not only for large banks but for also SMEs, may make banks less risk-averse in lending to these institutions.

I would like to end on a positive note. Just as there is a lot that Asia can learn from other regions, having worked at the IMF and compared countries across the globe—as you know, the IMF has 188 member countries—I would like to say that there is a lot that the rest of the world can learn from Asia.

After the Asian Financial Crisis, regulation and oversight were improved tremendously through reform of institutions and practices. These include supervision institutions, tighter loan classification, and capital requirement and bank restructuring. Asia has also since recently been a leader in implementing macro prudential policies that control or rein in macro-level risks through financial regulation. These reforms have indeed made Asian financial sectors much more resilient and have helped these economies avoid the worst financial effects after the Global Financial Crisis and have also helped them rebound rapidly.

So let us not underestimate the positive strides that Asia has made. Thank you.

Open Floor Discussion

Audience: Hi, I am with a financial institution here in Japan. I have questions for Dr. Muliaman, which might be related to the first point Mr. Ono mentioned. I 100 % agree on the importance of SMEs as a backbone of the economy and also to create some basis of employment. Actually, here in Japan the SMEs have been a big driver for economic growth for more than half a century. Here in Japan, banks of course provide those SME customers with financial access, but also sometimes introduce business opportunities to those customers. For instance, if there is an SME that produces a very unique machinery tool to enhance productivity, then banks may introduce those customers to bigger corporates to improve the efficiency of their production lines. We call that business matching. I think that Dr. Muliaman's comment on SME–large corporate linkage programs might stem from a similar idea.

So I would like to hear a little more about that program and also ask you if there is any room for foreign banks to make a contribution to that program? Thank you.

Jae-Ha Park: Yes, my question is to Dr. Hadad. As Mr. Kajikawa mentioned, he just provided a couple of interesting statistics on the kinds of vulnerabilities of some Asian countries, and also he mentioned the regional financial safety nets. Again, the tapering issue is coming to the fore, and some western countries and some Latin American countries again are showing some serious weaknesses in their financial sectors. I think these issues can be applied to any country in the Asian emerging economies.

As a person who is responsible for Indonesia's financial industry and financial stability, what are the current policy measures to cope with those kinds of shocks?

Muliaman Hadad: Thank you very much. My first comment is about policies on SMEs in Indonesia. I think Indonesia is one of many countries in Asia involved in SMEs for quite some time. We introduced a lot of initiatives during the last 25 years. And even up to now, in Indonesia they still lack the regulation that you have to lend at least 20 % of your lending portfolio to SMEs, so we still need to have a strong commitment basically to improve the access to finance for the SMEs.

Access to finance is not the only topic we have discussed so far. The low price of lending is also important. So easy access and the very high efficiency of the lending providers are very much the issues that I think will continue to be topical in the years to come.

On the linkage program you raised, we have been introducing these linkage initiatives I think for the last 5 years. We discussed the implementation of the linkage between banks and other financial institutions including microfinance or rural banks. One of the issues faced by micro banks or micro institutions or rural banks, as we call them, is liquidity. Then how to provide an appropriate access to liquidity for a small bank for the microfinance is really quite something, because they are really in the frontline dealing with access to finance issues, but then they are having liquidity issues because demand is very high. So then we proposed a kind of linkage with liquidity provided by bigger banks and then the smaller bank that are already on the front line basically in the rural areas can provide that lending for some additional activity. These are very much the issues.

For the last 5 years, it is very visible that a lot of newcomers are coming in to the SME focus of our banks. The banks are very focused, they are very committed. They are not only providing money, but they are also providing technical assistance, as you mentioned. Some of the banks in Indonesia change their offices into classrooms on Saturday and Sunday, bringing all their customers to the class on weekends. So this is very much the priority, but it is not easy.

We mentioned the importance of commitment and a good strategy because it is really quite a commitment to devise a clear strategy that includes providing technical assistance. These are very much the issues and I think we will continue to give direction.

My second comment is about stability. Indonesia is not the only country as far as the stability is concerned. For the last 12 months, perhaps we are dealing with the foreign currency exposures. Emerging markets, as mentioned earlier by Mr. Kajikawa, are exposed to global issues related to monetary policy tapering and things like that.

In terms of financial stability, Indonesia has two approaches. The first one is about financial stability prevention activities and the second about financial stability or instability resolution activities. So there are two parts to our financial stability approach. Regarding the prevention initiatives, we work very closely with the IMF and the World Bank in preventing vulnerabilities by improving, let us say, the quality of supervision, education, infrastructure, coordination, etc. I think it is really the general activities that we try to improve. We are also trying to improve what you might call crisis management protocols, as part of the crisis management resolution. It is part of the financial stability approach. We also work very closely with the other providers, the technical providers. We conduct what we call a fire drill exercise for tackling financial instability. Such exercises allow us to prepare for certain crisis scenarios. We simulate a range of scenarios, from very simple scenarios to very complicated scenarios.

In Indonesia, we established a Committee for Financial Stability, headed by the Minister of Finance and also including the Governor of the Central Bank, the Chairman of the Indonesia FSA, and the Chairman of the Deposit Insurance Corporation. We get together not only during times of distress, but also regularly in normal times, as part of our approach to ensuring financial stability.

I think that is my answer, thank you.

Masahiro Kawai: Thank you very much. I apologize that we have exceeded the allocated time and significantly so. But please join me in thanking all the panelists for excellent discussions.

References

Gill I, Kharas H (2007) An East Asian Renaissance: Ideas for Economic Growth. The World Bank, Washington, DC. pp. 17–18.

Closing Remarks

Masahiro Kawai

I am supposed to provide closing remarks. Given that we do not have any time left, I am not going to summarize today's discussion, except for pointing out several issues.

I think there was some concern about trade-offs among several issues. In the first session in the morning, there was discussion on financial stability and competition. There was a concern expressed that financial competition may lead to financial instability or at least may be a source of risk for financial stability. However, perhaps in this area, in my view, more empirical study would be needed about the relationship between competition and resulting financial sector efficiency versus financial stability.

In the second session, SME financing was discussed. I think there was tremendous consensus about what is needed to encourage SME financing. Strengthening the supporting infrastructure will be needed, reducing information asymmetry between SMEs and potential lenders. There is also a need to create an effective credit information system and minimize moral hazard in the event of credit guarantees, direct lending, and so forth.

On the issue of financial inclusion, financial education, and also financial stability, we saw a very interesting empirical study by ADBI staff. The conclusion was not conclusive, but I think the direction seems to be very good. I think discussing these issues from qualitative perspectives would be certainly very important, but a bit more empirical study is clearly needed.

Also, the need for financial education is extremely important in order to address not only financial inclusion, but in the era of financial sophistication I think financial education is becoming increasingly important. It concerns raising awareness about balancing risks and returns, and also awareness to choose from a set of financial products available in the market. Financial education has to be supported

---

M. Kawai
Asian Development Bank Institute, Tokyo, Japan

ADB Institute, Financial Services Agency, Japan, International Monetary Fund Regional Office for Asia and the Pacific (eds.), *Financial System Stability, Regulation, and Financial Inclusion,* ADB Institute Series on Development Economics, DOI 10.1007/978-4-431-55254-3_7

by policies to make the financial industry and financial products as transparent as possible.

Then, we just had a panel on Financing Asia's Growth. I think we learned a lot, such as that we need a more diversified financial market—not only banks, capital markets are certainly needed, and the expansion of capital markets can help the banking sector through securitization because of the need to continue to finance various types of investment. Making various types of financial products available to the market would be even more important.

My modest suggestion for the next year, if this conference continues, would be to take a look at more empirical data: To try to identify the statistical relationships among key measures, financial stability, financial competition, efficiency, inclusion, and maybe innovation also, rather than discussing these issues from qualitative perspectives, which are important, but I think it is time for all of us to take a look at more quantitative studies.

That is my modest suggestion for the next year. All of us, on behalf of the FSA, Japan, and the IMF, I would like to thank all the participants for coming, in particular from abroad, to attend this conference and contribute to this event in raising our awareness and interest in the issue of Asian finance. Thank you very much and I hope the foreign participants in particular will go home safely. Thank you very much, and also the audience for your generous time.

FSC
www.fsc.org
MIX
Papier | Fördert gute Waldnutzung
FSC® C083411

Kolibri 360 GmbH
Ferdinand-Jühlke-Straße 7
99095 Erfurt, Deutschland
produktsicherheit@kolibri360.de